Date Due

MAR 17			
JA 7 74			
MY 23 75			
DE			
MY 27 09			

Science and the Concept of Race

MARGARET MEAD, THEODOSIUS
DOBZHANSKY, ETHEL TOBACH,
& ROBERT E. LIGHT | EDITORS

SCIENCE AND THE
CONCEPT OF RACE

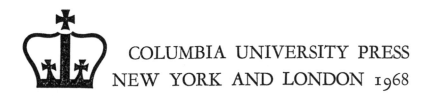

COLUMBIA UNIVERSITY PRESS
NEW YORK AND LONDON 1968

COPYRIGHT © 1968 COLUMBIA UNIVERSITY PRESS
LIBRARY OF CONGRESS CATALOG CARD NUMBER: 68–19754
PRINTED IN THE UNITED STATES OF AMERICA

PARTICIPANTS

PAUL T. BAKER, PH.D. Professor of Anthropology, Pennsylvania State University

HERBERT G. BIRCH, M.D., PH.D. Research Professor, Albert Einstein College of Medicine, Yeshiva University

THEODOSIUS DOBZHANSKY, D.SC. Professor of Biology and Genetics, Rockefeller University

LOREN EISELEY, PH.D. University Professor of Anthropology and the History of Science, University of Pennsylvania

MORTON H. FRIED, PH.D. Professor of Anthropology and Chairman of the Department, Columbia University

BENSON E. GINSBURG, PH.D. William Rainey Harper Professor of Biology, University of Chicago

BENTLEY GLASS, PH.D. Distinguished Professor of Biology and Academic Vice President, State University of New York at Stony Brook

EDMUND W. GORDON, ED.D. Professor of Educational Psychology and Guidance and Chairman of the Department, Ferkauf Graduate School, Yeshiva University

JERRY HIRSCH, PH.D. Professor of Psychology and Zoology, University of Illinois

DWIGHT J. INGLE, PH.D. Professor of Physiology and Chairman of the Department, University of Chicago

IRWIN KATZ, PH.D. Professor of Psychology, University of Michigan

PETER KILHAM Graduate Student, Department of Zoology, Duke University

PETER H. KLOPFER, PH.D. Associate Professor of Zoology, Duke University

WILLIAM S. LAUGHLIN, PH.D. Professor of Anthropology, University of Wisconsin

ROBERT E. LIGHT. Associate Director, Scientists' Institute for Public Information

GLORIA A. MARSHALL, PH.D. Assistant Professor of Anthropology, University of Michigan

ERNST MAYR, PH.D. Alexander Agassiz Professor of Zoology, Harvard University

MARGARET MEAD, PH.D. Curator of Ethnology, The American Museum of Natural History and Adjunct Professor of Anthropology, Columbia University

J. P. SCOTT, PH.D. Research Professor of Psychology, Bowling Green State University

ETHEL TOBACH, PH.D. Associate Curator, Department of Animal Behavior, The American Museum of Natural History

Foreword

Three decades ago when Adolf Hitler was declaiming his master race theories to the world, American scientists undertook to refute the Nazi nonsense and to insure that the public had some reasonable understanding of the concept of race. They made special efforts to reach the general public—through lectures and radio broadcasts and in articles, pamphlets, and books—to explain what science knew of race and its relevance to claims of innate superiority or inferiority of peoples. Much of this information found its way into the classroom. Students in the Thirties and Forties could explain with clarity such concepts as species, race, fertility, and hybridization.

Unfortunately, the level of information about race has declined sharply in this country. Today there are many foolish things said about race, and much of it by educated people. Ask a college student for a definition of race, and he will likely stammer out an incoherent answer; political leaders and many college professors will do no better. The mass media regularly misuse the term and disseminate misinformation. Americans are ignorant about race even while the amelioration of race relations is acknowledged as the nation's most immediate problem.

This situation prompted Scientists' Institute for Public Information (S.I.P.I.) to form a committee on biological and social aspects of race. S.I.P.I. directors Margaret Mead and Theodosius Dobzhansky were delegated to develop a public information program, and thus they set in motion the events that culminated in a symposium at the December, 1966 meetings of the American Association for the Advancement of Science.

This book is a reconstitution of that symposium. It is intended as an inventory of what science has to say about race. Some of the information is new; some of the articles are summaries of what science has learned over the years. The authors are from several academic disciplines, and they offer diverse views. We hope that the book will be of use in the classroom as well as in the private library and that it will encourage other discussions and the publication of other books. And we hope that these efforts will help to dispel the evil myths that persist about race.

Clearly, the organization of a three-session, nine-hour symposium, sponsored by six groups, and the translation of the proceedings into a book required extraordinary cooperation and forbearance by the participants. Particular acknowledgment is due Mrs. Cynthia Snow, who was a research assistant on the project and helped to edit the manuscript.

Robert E. Light

January, 1968

Contents

THREE. SOCIAL AND PSYCHOLOGICAL ASPECTS OF RACE

Science and the Concept of Race

MARGARET MEAD

Introductory remarks

This book is an outgrowth of a symposium held at the meetings of the American Association for the Advancement of Science in Washington on December 30, 1966. It gives an indication of the present state of knowledge and research on problems of race, and it represents a response to the barrage of pseudoscientific statements which, since the Supreme Court desegregation decision of 1954, have attempted to prove the innate biological inferiority of the group of Americans who are socially classified as Negro. These statements, which have drawn on inadequate, discredited, and inappropriate evidence to make blanket statements about the Negro, often carry the names of those who have held responsible academic positions; they include *The Biology of the Race Problem* by W. C. George (1), prepared by commission of the Governor of Alabama, *Race and Reason* by Carleton Putnam (2), and the pamphlet by Henry E. Garrett (3), "How Classroom Desegregation Will Work."

The response by members of the scientific community most concerned with problems of human biology and human cultural achievement has been confined almost entirely to blanket condemnations and repudiations of these anti-integration publications. One position or the other appears in scientific or popular journals or is invoked by the press, but on the whole the two positions never meet, and those opposing the Supreme Court decision continue to assert that there is sound scientific evidence that the American Negro has certain "racial" characteristics which make him the constitutional inferior of "white" Americans.

The social classification of Negroes—which the anti-integrationists try to buttress with biological arguments—is based on some known, often minute, attribute or visible amount of African ancestry. It ignores all other ancestries, whether European or Asian, so that Negro Ameri-

cans are treated sociologically and politically as if they are a race in the
sense that geographically isolated human populations can be spoken of as
races, as closed Mendelian populations. It ignores, too, the simplest logic
of genetics, which should attribute equal weight to paternal and maternal lines, recognize that individuals receive their particular genetic
characteristics from their particular parents and not from a population,
and that the attributed cultural achievements of African populations of
fifty thousand years ago are irrelevant to the potential behavior of children in the United States who happen to have some ancestry of African
origin.

There has been some improvement in public attitudes towards
race prejudice (4); however, new studies necessary to support the liber-
alized and more scientifically based arguments in favor of equal opportunity have been missing. At the same time there actually has been a
deterioration in the state of knowledge among educated laymen and
even among anthropologists on the subject of race differences. The discussion conducted in the pages of the international journal *Current
Anthropology* (5) in the early 1960s was scientifically inferior to the
arguments that were marshaled decades earlier in a period when biological knowledge was far less sophisticated.

In 1962 the American Anthropological Association officially re-
quested the American Association for the Advancement of Science
(AAAS) to investigate, on an interdisciplinary basis, whether there
was new evidence on racial differences which was relevant to the question of social and cultural achievement and full participation of Negroes
as citizens. The AAAS asked Dr. L. C. Dunn to conduct such an investigation. He reported that there was no new material on race differences
that would call into question the existing anthropological position on
the comparable capacities of all large-sized human populations. The
AAAS Committee on Science in the Promotion of Human Welfare then
made a statement to that effect in *Science* (6). The statement pointed
out the importance of the contribution of the social sciences but emphasized that those biological studies on race that could be successfully conducted had little relevance to the issue of any group's abilities to function successfully in society.

The Committee's position was challenged in the columns of *Science* by Drs. George and Garrett and Mr. Putnam (7). The opponents
of social measures to remove the barriers erected in our society against

the full participation of those who are sociologically classified as if they constitute a race—that highly diverse and hybridized group who are classified, and who classify themselves, as Negroes—continued to insist on using biological criteria in their interpretations of social and cultural data. They also insisted that evidence indicating a later date at which the use of fire was discovered in Africa is relevant to the achievements of individuals classified as Negro within our society and to records of performance tests when children classified as Negro are compared with children classified as "white." Clearly, the simple and monotonous repetition that there is no scientific evidence for this anti-integration position was not enough; nor was repeated reference to discussions written twenty-five years ago. It became increasingly obvious to those of us who were periodically drawn by public and private episodes into the conflict, as Dr. Dobzhansky and I have been, that this was a stalemate position.

A field in which no new research is being reported goes dead; both students and laymen feel that old knowledge couched in an out-of-date vocabulary must somehow be wrong and is at best unchallenging and uninteresting. When students ask what evidence there is on the question of hybrid vigor, for example, they are referred to the study of Bastards in Africa in 1913 (8) and to Dr. Harry Shapiro's classic study of the descendants of the mutineers of the Bounty made in 1923 (9). The literate lay public, which is exposed increasingly to new concepts of biology, has become more sophisticated on matters of blood types, pre-natal damage, Rh factors, and comparative animal behavior studies. They want to know what light these new studies throw on the question of racial differences.

The absence of fresh research on race can be attributed in part to political events of the last thirty years. In the Soviet Union there was the political suppression of evidence on genetic determination of characteristics of food plants in the Vavilov case (10) of the late 1930s and the political encouragement of Lysenkoism in the post-World War II period. The discussions on both sides of these conflicts were often gross violations of the scientific evaluation of evidence. The Nazi period with its racism and the murder of millions of Jews, Poles, and Gypsies was a greater deterrent to research on race differences and even proved a deterrent to research on constitutional differences and national character in which there was absolutely no invocation of race whatsoever (11). The ethically sensitive came to feel that in a world in which there was such gross and terrible misuse of attributed racial differences in capacity, research of any kind on differences which could be described as innate was likely to be misused. Many scientists, including anthropologists and psychologists, disapproved of all research on such differences. Those who either believed that socially significant race differences existed or wished to work on legitimate problems often felt that their research was disapproved of or discouraged.

It seemed that the whole area of science and race was appropriate for treatment by the science-information movement. The Scientists' Institute for Public Information (S.I.P.I.) is founded on the position that it is the scientist's duty to inform the public on the scientific aspects of major social issues, and not only to provide the information when asked but to initiate the communication. S.I.P.I. also takes the position that scientists have no greater competence than any other educated laymen on ultimate questions of political action, although they do have unique competence as well as unique responsibility where science itself is concerned. S.I.P.I.'s position on the ethical responsibility of scientists has evolved from the work begun in 1958 by local science-information committees, such as the St. Louis Committee for Environmental Information, in close conjunction with the AAAS Committee on Science in the Promotion of Human Welfare, partly through the active role played by Professor Barry Commoner in both.

Although the main focus of S.I.P.I. and the local information committees is on questions of contamination of the environment, they are also concerned with providing public information on other issues. At the 1965 S.I.P.I. meeting it was decided that a subcommittee on the biological and social aspects of race, with Dr. Dobzhansky and myself as co-chairmen, would explore the sort of material that would be needed if members of the local committees were to respond to requests for scientific information on the subject of race.

We recognized that the general public, partly of course in response to some of the propaganda about race but also quite practically responding to the multi-racial character of American origins and contemporary population, wants answers to biological questions. Interested laymen need to know what relevance, if any, experiments on early learning and animal behavior have for the kinds of learning that may be expected from different groups in different parts of the world.

They need to know the biological background and the biological implication of the intraspecies fertility of all human groups. They need
to know the implications of the persistence of a trait like sickle-cell
anemia in specific population groups after the eradication of malaria
has removed the advantages conferred on the heterozygotic members
of such a population. And because physique is of enormous importance
in parent-child, brother-sister, husband-wife relationships, they need to
know just what we do and do not know about hybridization.

Confronted with a world in which some of the constituent nations represent extremely divergent physical types and every level of
technological and socio-cultural development, all thinking persons
should know what, if any, is the connection between biologically given
physical characteristics and any kind of achievement. They need material which spells out the realities of cultural borrowing and diffusion
and the shifting content of socially and politically motivated attribu-
tions of superiority and inferiority. They need to know what the evidence is from studies of contemporary groups in the midst of change
in one generation, whether those concerned are Head Start children,
or competing national groups in modern Africa, or the just emerging
peoples of New Guinea.

However much those whose major concern is the prevention of
race prejudice may deny that there are races (12) or publish books
which fail to discuss physique (13), it remains true that physique still
occupies an important place in the public mind in connection with
decisions about school integration, fair-employment and housing laws,
and the repeal of anti-miscegenation laws. Where Americans of different ancestry—African, Amerindian, Asian—have been treated with
conspicuous and systematic discrimination, their positive achievements
and records of negative behavior differ from those of their majority
neighbors. These differences as well as the visible physical differences
arouse questions, and the questions have been met during the last two
decades by evasion and polemics on the integrationist side and by mis-
representation of scientific findings, legalisms, and polemics on the
anti-integrationist side.

While the whole operation of caste and class distinctions in society is the area of competence of social scientists, the points of articu-
lation between hereditary characteristics and social classification, where
biology and the social sciences meet, are also very important. We are

convinced that unless there is a continuous interdisciplinary exchange on the new and exciting findings in genetics, psychology, anthropology, and sociology and a consciousness of their relevance to the widespread social changes going on in society, a kind of paralysis falls upon our thinking.

It is with these concerns in mind that this symposium was organized. It was originally conceived as Parts Two and Three of the present book, to be cosponsored by the Scientists' Institute for Public Information and the AAAS Committee on Science in the Promotion of Human Welfare. When we found that Dr. Tobach was independently organizing Part One to highlight the relationship of studies in comparative animal behavior with an understanding of racial problems, the two symposium plans were combined. The interdisciplinary sponsorship was broadened to include AAAS Sections F, H, and I—respectively Zoological Sciences, Anthropology, and Psychology—and the Animal Behavior Society to further underline our concern with the need for new research and clarification in this whole area of race.

REFERENCES

1. Wesley C. George, *The Biology of the Race Problem* (Birmingham, Ala., 1962).
2. Carleton Putnam, *Race and Reason* (Washington, Public Affairs Press, 1961).
3. Henry E. Garrett, *How Classroom Desegregation Will Work* (Richmond, Va., Patrick Henry Press).
4. See, for example, H. H. Remmers and D. H. Radler, *The American Teenager* (Indianapolis, Bobbs-Merrill Co., Inc., 1957).
5. *Current Anthropology*, 3 (1962); 4 (1963); 5 (1964).
6. AAAS Committee on Science in the Promotion of Human Welfare, "Science and the Race Problem," *Science*, 142 (1963), 558–61.
7. Carleton Putnam, "Science and the Race Problem," *Science*, 142 (1963), 1419–20, and Henry E. Garrett and Wesley C. George, "Science and the Race Problem," *Science*, 143 (1964), 913–15.
8. Eugen Fischer, *Die Rehobother Bastards und das Bastardierungsproblem beim Menschen. Anthropologische und ethnographische Studien am Rehobother Bastardvolk in Deutsch-Südwest-Africa* (Jena, G. Fischer, 1913).

9. Harry L. Shapiro, "Descendants of the Mutineers of the Bounty," *Memoirs of the Bernice P. Bishop Museum* (Honolulu, The Museum, 1929), II.

10. Conway Zirkle, ed., *Death of a Science in Russia* (Philadelphia, University of Pennsylvania Press, 1949).

11. J. M. Tanner, "Growth and Constitution," in A. L. Kroeber, ed., *Anthropology Today* (Chicago, University of Chicago Press, 1953), 750–70, and H. C. J. Duijker and N. H. Frijda, *National Character and National Stereotypes* (Amsterdam, North-Holland Publishing Co., 1960).

12. Ashley Montagu, "Antidote to Barbarism," *The Saturday Review of Literature*, 33 (August 19, 1950), 8–9 and 38–40.

13. Edgar T. Thompson and Everett C. Hughes, eds., *Race: Individual and Collective Behavior* (New York, The Free Press, 1958).

ONE ✵ BEHAVIOR-GENETIC ANALYSES AND THEIR RELEVANCE TO THE CONSTRUCT OF RACE

ETHEL TOBACH

Introduction

At this year's AAAS meeting we are being asked to consider the most advanced technological manipulations of the physical aspect of man's environment. We recognize that these changes have also affected man's social environment and his behavior. Old knowledge about the world in which he lives is being replaced, along with old ways of thinking about other people and the worlds in which they live.

Within the category of man's social behavior, there are many levels of organization of experience. As the individual child develops, concepts relevant to social organization, such as family, friend, nation, and, in many instances, race, become part of his thinking. The ideas of nation and race have been predominant in the history of conflict among men for control of natural resources. These categories of nation and race are rather old, but the discoveries of evolution and genetics gave new sources of energy to those who traditionally find it useful to misapply the findings of experimental investigations based on scientific theories. These discoveries have also allowed us to see man in relationship to other animals, and the study of infrahuman animals has contributed to our understanding of man—his ecology, his physiology, and his behavior. The study of his own behavior has been most difficult. Scientific method demands the examination of the criteria used to determine the biases which may have entered into the collection of facts —the well-known problem of experimental control. These criteria must also be understood by the public in its interpretation of the studies. The findings of the animal behaviorists have been most misused in this respect.

The animal behaviorist asks comparative questions about human and infrahuman behavior and frequently finds that the answers he obtains are used in various ways by other people. He has little control

13

over how these facts are used, as is the case with other scientists. His work is cited to substantiate strategies and tactics of conflicting ideologies and philosophies for conducting the life of man, whether in regard to child-rearing, group relations, or problems of war and peace.

The papers in this section deal with the attempts of animal behaviorists to delimit the relationships of the biochemical codings and processes we call genetics, behavior and environmental factors. The papers raise several questions: What is the proper formulation of questions about these relationships? What are the limits of the interpretation of the answers to these questions? What new problems are raised by these answers? And, finally, what is their relevance to human behavior?

Kilham and Klopfer's study is an example of one method animal behaviorists use to elucidate the relationship of species-typical (genetic) characteristics and environmental experience to social behavior. The three other papers are theoretical and differ in many important conceptual respects as well as in focus. As we examine these carefully considered statements, we are fully aware that the discussion of race in the market place is seldom logically calculated. There are those who plead for the elimination of the term for that reason. Others see this solution as a denial of the freedom of scientific research. Dr. Hirsch's solution to this dilemma is to show that it stems from the formulation of a pseudo problem, that is, the heredity-environment dichotomy. On the basis of other theoretical considerations, Dr. Birch gives additional experimental evidence to support the position that this formulation is fallacious.

The nature-nurture dichotomy is the theoretical basis for much of the research on biologically defined racial phenomena. The thesis that the dichotomy creates more difficulties than it solves is supported by the concept of levels of integration. The attitude-ridden concepts of "race" pertain to the level of human social behavior. This level integrates some of its unique qualities from preceding levels of biochemical and physiological levels of organization. Other behavioral phenomena of the level of human organization, such as thought and communication, have their *anlage* in the behavior of earlier animal forms but differ importantly in such typically human processes as symbolic thinking, speech, and cultural history. Each level of organization requires its own constructs and techniques and subsumes within itself lower, less complex levels. The use of the concept of race by biologists to deal with differences between populations of organisms and differences between individuals is not universally acceptable. At the lowest level of contention, it may be acceptable when applied to a level of organization other than that of *human behavior*.

The contribution of the animal behaviorist lies not only in his experimental findings but also in the profound recognition of this evolutionary concept as it applies to behavior. Implicit in this comparative approach is the expectation and realization that problems on lower levels are increasingly compounded on higher levels. This is true both for levels within the individual, for example, the relevance of biochemical transport at neuronal membranes and feeding behavior, and for levels of organization among individuals, for example, phyletic differences in feeding behavior.

PETER KILHAM AND PETER H. KLOPFER

The construct race and the innate differential

"Groups of actually or potentially interbreeding populations which are reproductively isolated from other such groups": this is the classical definition of a species, as given by Mayr (1), and the only definition of operational value. Within a species there may be subgroups between which gene flow is particularly enhanced or retarded because of geographic propinquity, behavioral differences, or, particularly in human beings, social or economic factors. Subgroups of a species may pass under many names: variety is one, race another. Some authors have attempted to use different names to distinguish degrees of genetic distinctiveness. Such an effort is at best an arbitrary exercise; at worst, it poses the danger of confusing the older, pre-Darwinian typological taxa with taxa as defined today. It is no less a risk, however, to take an opposite tack and fail altogether to acknowledge the existence of local eddies in the gene pool. Buettner-Janusch (2) writes:

> Those who hold the "races don't exist" point of view are exasperated by the inadequacy and inconsistency of published classifications, by the evils of bigotry, and by the boresomeness of most writing on race. Their hearts are in the right place, but their heads are not. Partisans in each camp confuse the analytical categories—the taxa of a classification—with real biological events. They mix up statements of politics, ethics, genetics, anthropology, and civil rights. . . .

This work was supported by NIMH Grant 04453 and a Career Development Award to Peter H. Klopfer. We are grateful to Mr. James Potter and Mrs. Catherine Dewey for technical assistance and to Jeremy J. Hatch for his critical suggestions.

16

Race is a perfectly useful and valid term. . . . [It] is a Mendelian population, a reproductive community of individuals
sharing a common gene pool. *The level at which the reproductive community is defined depends upon the problem one is interested in investigating. There is no absolute, final, or "true"
level at which these reproductive communities are defined.*
[Italics ours]

Buettner-Janusch was addressing his remarks to anthropologists
concerned with the races of mankind. His comments apply with equal
force to students of animals other than man. Unfortunately, such comments have often gone unheard. A recent issue of a scientific journal,
for example, contained a paper on the structure of the salt gland of "the
duck." Nowhere in this detailed description of a small bit of tissue was
there reference to the kind of duck or the region whence it came: a
singular shortcoming in view of the variations in size and function of
salt glands between marine and fresh-water races of ducks.

For domestic strains or races, the selection exercised by man has
usually been deliberate: leghorn fowl were selected for egg production,
elkhounds for hunting bear and moose. Where studies of animals have
involved the characteristics on which selection was focused, the authors
have shown sensitivity to the genetic status of the subjects. However,
cognizance has not always been taken of less obvious side effects or
pleiotropisms; sometimes these subtly affect perceptual mechanisms and
gross interpretative errors may result, no less disastrous than those from
studies of the salt glands of "the duck." Who would have guessed, as
Wecker's data now suggest (3), that the prairie and woodland races
of the deer mouse, *Peromyscus maniculatus*, differ in their ability to be
imprinted upon their characteristic habitat? A classic example of this
"innate differential," of course, is afforded by Howells and Vine (4).
They demonstrated that domestic chicks can more readily learn a discrimination when the cue is provided by a member of the chick's own
strain* than when it is provided by one of a different strain—in this
case, bantams and leghorns. In short, they showed that genetic isolation
can and does lead to important differences even between members of
the same species. This subject merits attention, despite the social dan-

---

* Let it not be forgotten that domestic strains or races are in their degree of
genetic similarity more nearly equivalent to siblings, even twins, than to human
races.

gers that lie in unjustified extrapolations to man and to his political
and social rights. The facility with which bigots can obscure this fact
must not blind us, in turn, to the consequences of genetic isolation and
racial differentiation.

The study we have undertaken was designed (I) to test the
validity of the Howells and Vine conclusions, that there are strain
differences in perceptual preferences in chicks (II) to identify the relevant cues by which the subjects make the requisite discriminations, and,
finally (III) to discover how apparently innate perceptual preferences
are programmed by the nervous system. For example, if the discrimination between own-strain and alien-strain is based on color (but we do
not here present evidence that this is so), is this due to differential
distribution of retinal oil droplets, to sensitivity of retinal cells (periph-
eral filtering), or to central mechanisms? Since we have just begun this
work, we will report here only the results of Study I, as thus far com-
pleted. The study of the relevant cues, such as sound, movement, and
color, will be presented elsewhere.

METHODS

The technique adopted involved giving the subjects, newly
hatched chicks, a choice between approaching one of their own or one
of an alien kind. The apparatus consisted of a circular arena, 120 cm
in diameter, with a wall 50 cm high (Figure 1). It was painted a uni-

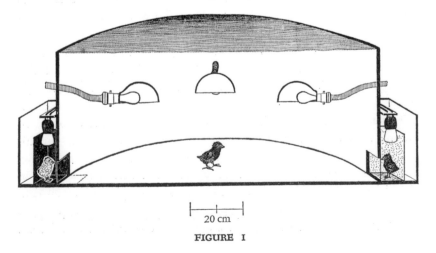

|———|———|
20 cm

FIGURE I

form gray. On opposite sides of the arena were two clear plastic observation windows (9 by 13 cm), behind each of which was a lighted
chamber (13 by 9 cm) containing the "observed" animal. Lighting of
the central arena was provided by four 25-watt incandescent bulbs located 30 cm above the arena and 30 cm from its wall. Each observation
chamber was lighted with one 10-watt incandescent bulb, 15 cm above
the floor. The entire apparatus was covered by cheesecloth and placed
in a darkened room to prevent the subjects from seeing the experimenter.
The ambient temperature was kept at 21°C.

The subjects consisted of Vantress-cross (yellow) chicks and sex-
link (black) chicks. They were communally hatched in our darkened
laboratory incubators and held there, in the dark, for an additional 24–
30 hours. Thirty minutes (approximately) before testing, each chick
was individually placed in an open cardboard compartment, 12 cm
square, and held under an incandescent bulb to accustom it to light,
thereby reducing fear responses during testing.

Experiment I: Preferences of naive chicks

The apparatus was prepared for the experiment by placing a
Vantress chick in one observation chamber and a sex-link chick in the
other. The Vantress observed chicks were placed against a black background, and the sex-link observed chicks against a white background.
[In a separate experiment (III) the influence of the background was
examined.] A subject that had previously had no visual experience (except for the solitary half-light adjustment period) was placed in the
center of the apparatus facing away from the observation windows and
was then allowed to wander freely throughout the arena. A choice was
recorded if the chick spent 2 minutes continuously within 6 cm of the
observation window and exchanged pecks with the observed chick
through the window. The test session was terminated either after the
chick made a choice or after 10 minutes, if no choice had been made.
All subject chicks were returned to the incubator after their exposure
to the apparatus, and a sample of the original number was retested 12
hours later to determine the reliability of the original choice.

Experiment II: Preferences of socialized chicks

1. Within 6 hours after hatching, the subject chicks were placed
in separate lighted cardboard compartments containing another chick of

the same age, which served as a social *Kumpan*. The two chicks were left together for 24–30 hours before being placed individually in the apparatus and tested, as described above. In half of the trials the subjects were of the same strain (*a*), and in half of different strains (*b*).

2. In these experiments the chicks were given an equal exposure to chicks of their own and an alien strain. They were held, as above, but in groups of 4–2 chicks of each strain—then tested in the usual manner.

Experiment III: Effects of the background

The same procedure as employed in II was adopted here with the following differences: (*a*) the socialization sessions involved only Vantress chicks, and (*b*) the tests were conducted with Vantress chicks serving as observed chicks in both chambers, one against a white, the other against a black, background.

About 400 subjects, approximately 80 in each experiment, served for this study. Analysis of the data was based on the chi square.

RESULTS

Experiment I showed that neither group (Vantress or sex-link) of naive chicks had a preference for one or the other of the two observed animals (Table 1). Experiment II-1*a* showed that chicks of

TABLE 1: EXPERIMENT I
PREFERENCES OF NAIVE CHICKS

| Group | Preferences | | No Choice | Level of Probability, χ^2 |
	Yellow	Black		
Yellow	16	17	7	$.80 < P < .90$
Black	20	15	5	$.30 < P < .50$

both varieties, when communally reared with their own kind, developed a strong preference for the observed chick of their variety (Table 2). Chicks which were reared with the alien variety (Experiment II-1*b*) failed to show such a preference (Table 3). Chicks simultaneously

reared with both varieties (Experiment II-2) still preferred their own kind (Table 4).

TABLE 2: EXPERIMENT II-1*a*
PREFERENCES OF CHICKS SOCIALIZED WITH OWN KIND

Group	Preferences		No Choice	Level of Probability, χ^2
	Yellow	*Black*		
Yellow	26	4	10	$P < .001$
Black[a]	6	41	25	$P < .001$

[a] Pooled data from three trials, the differences between which were statistically insignificant ($.30 < P < .50$).

TABLE 3: EXPERIMENT II-1*b*
PREFERENCES OF CHICKS SOCIALIZED WITH ALIEN KIND

Group	Preferences		No Choice	Level of Probability, χ^2
	Yellow	*Black*		
Yellow	13	18	9	$.30 < P < .50$
Black	18	14	3	$.30 < P < .50$

TABLE 4: EXPERIMENT II-2
PREFERENCES OF CHICKS SOCIALIZED WITH BOTH VARIETIES

Group	Preferences		No Choice	Level of Probability, χ^2
	Yellow	*Black*		
Yellow	21	5	29	$P < .005$
Black	0	15	27	$P < .001$

The chicks used in Experiments I and II were retested after 24 hours. The naive chicks of Experiment I showed no consistency in their preferences, while the socialized chicks of Experiment II retained their original preferences. Table 5 compares the preferences shown by chicks in the original experiment with the preferences that the chicks showed when retested. The values reported in this table represent pooled data for Vantress and sex-link chicks since the differences between these groups were statistically insignificant ($.20 < P < .30$, χ^2 and $.30 < P < .50$, χ^2).

TABLE 5

COMPARISON OF PREFERENCES SHOWN BY CHICKS IN THE ORIGINAL EXPERIMENTS WITH THE PREFERENCES THE CHICKS SHOWED WHEN RETESTED

| | Comparison of Preferences | | Level of |
Experiment	Unchanged	Changed	Probability, χ^2
I. Naive Chicks	21 (exp 20)	19 (exp 20)	.70 < P < .80
II. Yellow Chicks	39 (exp 21)	3 (exp 21)	P < .001

Experiment III was designed to test whether or not the color (white or black) of the background behind the "observed" chicks affected the preferences revealed in the other experiments (Table 6).

TABLE 6: EXPERIMENT III

PREFERENCES OF CHICKS SOCIALIZED WITH OWN KIND, AGAINST DIFFERENT BACKGROUNDS

| | Preferences | | | |
Group	Black Background	White Background	No Choice	Level of Probability, χ^2
Yellow	19	16	5	.50 < P < .70

The chicks did not appear to have any background preference.

During each experiment we noted that some of the chicks showed a "fear" response, characterized by closing their eyes, bobbing their heads, and often dropping their beaks to the floor. Some other chicks ran back and forth across the apparatus in an apparently aimless fashion. Chicks showing either of these responses have been pooled under the heading "No Choice" in the tables.

DISCUSSION

The absence of any clear and consistent preference of chicks for others of the same variety before social contact with other chicks is not of itself surprising. What is unexpected is that experience with chicks of the alien variety does not lead to the aliens being preferred. It is as

if the chick is so designed that a *particular* experience is prerequisite
to the establishment of a perceptual preference (preferring own-kind).
Presumably, other experiences (for example, contact with alien chicks)
are barred by a perceptual filter or, alternatively, only certain perceptual preferences are immanent: while these still require activation to
be manifest, other kinds of preferences cannot be similarly established.
Such a result is not unique to this experiment; indeed, it is probably
a very common situation whose importance has been all but lost in the
traditional instinct-learning controversy (5). For instance, consider
Wecker's (3) important study of habitat selection in deer mice (*Peromyscus* species). A laboratory-reared strain of mice derived from a field-
dwelling race showed no strong preference for a field over a woods
habitat. By rearing some young in each of these two habitats, Wecker
established that an experience in the field early in life could produce
a preference for that habitat. However, a similar experience in a wood
did not produce a corresponding preference for the forest habitat. Here,
too, the preference for fields was immanent in the sense that a particular experience was required in order for a response (choice of field over
forest) to be elicited; a different experience could not elicit a different
preference, however. Presumably, deer mice derived from the forest-
dwelling races could only be "trained" to prefer the wooded habitat,
but this experiment has yet to be performed.

In studies of imprinting, Klopfer and Hailman (6) and Klopfer
(7) found a similar situation, though, as will be seen, with one important difference.

Initially, we merely demonstrated that the exposure to a moving
model during the critical period was indeed necessary if our
subjects (domestic Vantress-cross chicks and domestic Pekin
ducklings) were to show the following-response outside of the
critical period. We then divided our experimental animals into
two groups; individuals of each group were exposed to one or the
other of two models during the critical period. One of these
models was a white *papier-mâché* mallard decoy (plain model);
the other was an identical decoy that was painted a variety of
bright colors [striking model]. Twenty-four hours after the original exposure the animals were allowed a simultaneous choice
between the two models. They chose to follow the brightly

colored model regardless of which of the two they had originally been exposed to. It must be emphasized that during the initial exposure, both models, the plain and the colored, had elicited the same [degree of] following from the same number of chicks or ducklings.

We interpreted the foregoing to mean that the imprinting experience—that is, the exposure to a model during the critical period—served merely to activate the following-response. The preferred characteristics of the object being followed were apparently fixed in some other way, presumably independently of the visual experience of the subjects.

These are intriguing systems in which preferences do not appear except in the presence of a specific stimulus (just how specific remains to be seen).

The importance of a perceptual bias is further indicated by the Howells and Vine results (4). The preferential learning which is the consequence of the initial bias amplifies the original effect. To determine both the degree and the character of further amplification will prove to be as interesting as to determine the sensory and neural basis of the bias itself. For our immediate purposes, the point of greatest relevance to this symposium is that this result, which is of such considerable theoretical significance, is largely dependent on the recognition and differentiation of taxa below the level of the species. For students of behavior, the construct "race" cannot be ignored.

SUMMARY

Naive chicks, whether of a yellow or a black variety, show no consistent tendency to approach other chicks of the same variety; when communally reared in the light with chicks of their own variety they do develop a preference for their own kind. However, when reared with chicks of the alien variety, no consistent preferences appear. Preferences for own-kind are immanent but require activation by a particular experience. Programming of perceptual systems so that an experience is prerequisite to a response, but with only certain kinds of experiences or responses being possible, seems to be an important feature of organisms.

REFERENCES

1. Ernst Mayr, *Animal Species and Evolution* (Cambridge, Mass., Belknap Press, 1963).
2. John Buettner-Janusch, review of Carleton S. Coon's, *The Living Races of Man* in *American Journal of Physical Anthropology,* n.s., 25 (1966), 182–88.
3. S. C. Wecker, "The Role of Early Experience in Habitat Selection by the Prairie Deer Mouse," *Ecological Monographs,* 33 (1963), 307–25.
4. Thomas H. Howells and Donald O. Vine, "The Innate Differential in Social Learning," *Journal of Abnormal and Social Psychology,* 35 (1940), 537–48.
5. Peter H. Klopfer and J. P. Hailman, *An Introduction to Animal Behavior: Ethology's First Century* (Englewood Cliffs, N. J., Prentice-Hall, 1967).
6. Peter H. Klopfer and J. P. Hailman, "Perceptual Preferences and Imprinting in Chicks," *Science,* 145 (1964), 1333–34.
7. Peter H. Klopfer, "Imprinting: A Reassessment," *Science,* 147 (1965), 302–3.

BENSON E. GINSBURG AND
WILLIAM S. LAUGHLIN

The distribution of genetic differences in behavioral potential in the human species

The topic of the symposium, "The Utility of the Construct of Race," appears to invite us to choose sides, or at least to vote *yes* or *no* regarding the usefulness of this concept. However, the topics of the three sessions of the symposium—"Behavior-Genetic Analyses and Their Relevance to the Construct of Race," "Biological Aspects of Race in Man," and "Social and Psychological Aspects of 'Race'"—tell us that the rubric "race" and the various concepts with which it has been identified are with us, have been with us, and will continue to be with us, whatever euphemisms we may attempt to substitute for the controversial four-letter word, and however much we may deplore the political, cultural, and biological misuses to which it has been subjected. We should remind ourselves that the term *race* does not have a merely human connotation. There are races of fruit flies, mice, and plants. As Professor Dobzhansky has pointed out elsewhere in this symposium, if there were no such construct, we should have had to invent it in order

The authors gratefully acknowledge the support of several NIH and NIMH grants supporting their individual research, and that of the Center for Advanced Study in the Behavioral Sciences, which made their study and collaboration possible.

26

to account for local genetic differences between population groups which are only partially isolated from each other and continue to exchange genes but also to maintain some obvious differences. It is our concern to demonstrate that current evidence must be interpreted as indicating that behavioral equipotentiality exists for all such populations of reasonable size and that populations can direct their areas of biological achievement by internal genetic restructuring. Behavioral and social forces that direct such restructuring constitute the major selective agencies determining the further evolution of the human species.

The human species is not panmictic and was undoubtedly less so in the past than it is today. Its subpopulations are separated by barriers of distance, geography, language, religion, and a host of other cultural customs, ensuring that now, as in the past, the total species remains a breeding reticulum composed of partial isolates within which there is significantly more genetic exchange than there is between component groups, some of which are as recognizably different from each other as are races, breeds, and varieties of other species. Physically we come packaged in a range of colors and a variety of body types. Particular clusters of these attributes are not randomly distributed, but, rather, differentiate Eskimos from American Indians from Indian Indians from a variety of Mongolian types, a myriad of Negro types, and a diversity of Caucasoids. We do not dismiss or minimize these physical differentiators—and could not if we would. They serve primarily as convenient external markers by which we identify individuals and classify populations.

The identifying hallmarks differentiating component populations within the human species are more than skin deep. They extend to skeletal structures, blood groups, the prevalence of various abnormalities such as sickle-cell anemia, Tay-Sachs disease, and favism, and if we are to be quantitative rather than qualitative, to a variety of physiological, clinical, and behavioral measures.

Man is not unique in these respects. Physical, physiological, and behavioral differences have been described for subpopulations within many other well-studied animal species. In fact, it would be nothing short of remarkable if we were to find that the Ainu and the Zulu were alike in their genetic capacities and therefore in their morphological, physiological, and behavioral characteristics. There is neither a moral nor a scientific dilemma, so far as the physical attributes are concerned, as no superiority or inferiority inheres in skin color, hair texture, or body conformation, *per se*, throughout the normal range of variation. Nor do we pretend that there is genetic egalitarianism with respect to the way these properties are distributed among the various "races" within the human species. Despite demonstrations that there are dietary effects on growth and hormonal effects on pigment, we find no need to place exaggerated emphasis upon these environmental contributions to differences in stature or skin color, or to denigrate the biological components of these aspects of phenotype.

When it comes to physiological, biochemical, or immunological differences, we are similarly unconcerned from a moral or sociological point of view. When it comes to differences in behavioral potential, however, the issues suddenly become explosive to the point where the mere admission of the possibility of comparable biological differences in this realm becomes, not an object for discussion and scientific study, but one for moral censure and apologistic adventurism.

We suspect, therefore, that there are two avenues open to those working in behavior genetics and biological anthropology. One avenue is to maintain (as some anthropologists have) that biologically based differences in behavioral capacities are superficial, and that all important human behavioral capacities are so fundamental to the entire species that all subgroups share these as a common evolutionary heritage. On this view, individual differences in behavioral capacities within races of moderate to large population size constitute an adequate sample of the totality of human behavioral variation, and significant differences in the behavioral realm between human ethnic groups are therefore culturally determined. Genetic differences could have been obtained only by sustained differential selection, and proponents of the view that there are no important biological differences in behavioral capacities between diverse human population groups generally argue that selection for behavioral differences would have had to be intense, consistent, and of long duration to accomplish such a result. They maintain that this has not been the case; they are critical of the possibility that important sampling differences may have occurred; and they "explain" any seemingly contradictory data on the basis of cultural determination.

A second avenue is provided by the argument that animal data, for one reason or another, may not have relevance to man, since human

data rest on such a complex of nature-nurture interactions in which
nature is represented by an unanalyzable polygenic system, that no
analyses on human populations in this area are presently meaningful.
Many social anthropologists, sociologists, and educators make the further argument that nature is something we can do nothing about, while
we have only begun to scratch the surface of what can be accomplished
by manipulating cultural, social, and psychological variables, and that
these, therefore, represent the hopeful frontiers of research. Behavioral
genetic research on the human species, they say, is premature and, moreover, dangerous, since it lends itself to a racist point of view and is,
therefore, inimical to any civilized concept of human rights and elementary political or personal decency.

We are here to argue that, if anything, the reverse is true. The
pretenders to having cultural equalizing devices go far beyond their
data in offering these as panaceas. In fact, recognition of genetic inequalities in behavior potential within the different breeding partial
isolates of the human species and characterization of these differences
permit us to both maximize the behavioral endowments we possess and
offer the major scientific hope for upgrading our biological condition.
We are not here considering the yet unrealized possibility of rewriting
the DNA code script in such a way as to correct for genetic deficiencies
at the molecular source. Neither are we arguing that groups need to
share their genetic endowments by interbreeding in order to achieve
behavioral parity—a notion which assumes the inherent superiority of
one group over another and seeks to upgrade the "inferior" groups by
introducing more favorable genes from a better endowed population.
The gist of the genetic argument is quite different and entails no need
for looking at things other than as they are in order to point the way
clearly toward making them more nearly as we wish they were.

Behavior genetic analyses have demonstrated the following relevant facts:

1. A measure of central tendency with respect to a behavioral
attribute of a genetically variable group provides very little useful information. The isomorphism of the attribute being measured with the
way in which the organism's behavioral capacities are organized is not
to be inferred from the fact that members within a given population
can be measured in this particular respect. Individuals graded alike on
such a measure may yet be genetically different with respect to the

behavioral potential the test purports to measure. In genetic terms, the attribute may be only one aspect of a natural phenotype, or may confound overlapping regions between a variety of such phenotypes as well as confound a phenotype with its phenocopy. Moreover, even if the attribute tested corresponded to the natural organization of behavioral capacities, there is more than one genetic way to a given phenotype, as well as a variety of nongenetic routes to a phenocopy (1, 2).

2. While it is true that behavior is complicated, and that behavioral capacities are likely to be affected by many genes, it does not follow that the genetic substratum for such capacities are unanalyzable or that particular major genes do not exert major determining influences on these capacities or potentials.

3. Many seemingly highly correlated phenomena have no necessary causal connections so that data demonstrating correlations among physical, physiological, and behavioral attributes in particular populations must be further interpreted in order to evaluate the significance of the correlations obtained (3).

In order to demonstrate the relevance of these three desiderata for the topic in question, we should like to cite several examples from the behavioral realm.

Strain differences in susceptibility to sound-induced seizures in mice have been heavily researched by a number of laboratories for more than three decades (4, 5, 6, 7, 8, 9). A variety of genetic hypotheses have been offered, ranging from monogenic determination to complex polygenic models for this easily recognizable phenotype. Every important neural transmitter and several hormones have been correlated with this behavior. A number of pigment genes also have been shown to be associated with it. The periods of maximum susceptibility for a given strain or genotype have been authoritatively but variously described—all this with exactly the same strains (members of which are very nearly genetic replicates) under comparable conditions of rearing and testing. Strain differences in aggressiveness of male mice have also been reliably differentiated, with similar remarkable differences in results (1, 10). In both these cases, and in many others, further analytic work has demonstrated that there are individual major genic differences contributing to the characteristics in question and that these can be analyzed one at a time in terms of some of their intermediary metabolic and physiological effects, which may then, in turn, be related to the behavioral capacities (1, 2). Each genetic substitution can be put on a variety of different inbred strain backgrounds, so that interaction effects may also be studied. These interactions account for differences in scaling and timing, and for some of the other seeming discrepancies in the earlier literature. It is possible also to demonstrate, by this precise genetic methodology, that some of the correlations with pigment genes, neural transmitter levels, and endocrine factors result from linkage or other noncausal associations, while others are not dissociable from the genetic substitution and must be considered to be causally related to the differences in behavior under study. Through the identification of some of the gene-controlled mechanisms, the "natural phenotype" can be inferred. In the examples analyzed by this method, the phenotype is invariably broader than the original attribute discovered from either observation or testing.

Differences in results on mouse strain aggressiveness are particularly instructive because some can be resolved by instituting different treatments in the very early pre-weaning period. How animals respond to a variety of handling and other regimes, and when they are maximally responsive to such treatments, is a function of strain and, therefore, of genotype (1). Similar differences in aggressiveness and emotionality in relation to early handling paradigms have been reported for various breeds of dogs (11). Selection experiments with both mice and dogs have demonstrated that it is possible to affect behavioral capacities profoundly within 7 to 10 generations, and that this can be achieved from an initial population that has been selected to quite a different set of behavioral criteria, if this base population is genetically variable (3, 10). In these instances, phenotypic selection for the first set of criteria included a variety of genetic ways of arriving at the phenotype in a normative spectrum of environmental conditions. Selection not only can move the population to a new phenotypic norm without resorting to crosses with outside individuals but it also can repackage the behavioral and morphological attributes so that a particular color type and body conformation that was previously associated with a given constellation of behavioral characters, either by accident or selection, can later become associated with quite a different behavioral profile (12).

If these arguments are extended to the human species, similar inferences may be drawn despite the broader behavioral lability and the obviously greater effects of experiential factors. Differences in sensitive periods for response to stress as well as the effects of such early stimulation on the direction and magnitude of later emotional behavior rest on homologies of mechanisms that can be investigated, as well as on analogies of behavioral effects. Differences in intelligence (however we may parse its constituent capacities), in perceptual abilities, musical ability, mathematical ability, and many other aspects of human achievement and performance show high heritability (13). While it is obvious that individuals placed in environments where these capacities are undetected and unnurtured may never exhibit their potential, the converse is also true.

The search for meaningful behavioral phenotypes in human populations, which has leaned heavily on sibship and twin data, must be expanded to include a comparative study of the entire species and especially of small population isolates in which there is appreciable consanguinity. Such isolates may be expected to provide a variety of samples from the total gene pool and to favor the expression of various recessive and otherwise buffered genes. Most such studies have thus far included relatively narrow samples of behavioral attributes.

It would seem, by analogy with animal experiments, including homologies of structure and mechanism, that human behavioral phenotypic variability is affected by many genetic factors and that the human genome, no less than the nonhuman, has ensured itself of a variety of pathways to similar behavioral capacities. The inference that follows from the genetic dissimilarities in behavior potential among the diverse populations comprising the human species is not that these differences, which inhere in the populations, cannot be bridged without an exchange of genes, but rather that a tremendous amount of genetic variability with respect to behavioral potential has been assimilated to a much narrower range of phenotypic expression. Many of these differences can be detected and magnified by cultural devices, which also affect the structuring of the gene pool, whether or not genetic exchange between population groups is involved.

Teleologically speaking, it is advantageous for a population to contain a high amount of genetic variability, as this represents the future evolutionary potential of the species. Wright has estimated that such genotypic variability may amount to an average of ten alleles for each genetic locus (14). The process of biparental reproduction magnifies this variability exponentially by recombining the genetic constellations that may occur in a large, random-breeding population in proportion to the frequency of occurrence of each allele, restricted by the phenomenon of linkage, expanded by the process of mutation, and guided by natural selection (14). Natural selection can act only indirectly to modify the frequency of a given gene through the average fitness of the phenotypes that result from its occurrence over a range of combinations with other genes. If each unique genetic combination expressed itself equivalently on a scale of equal increments, the phenotypic variability for each genetically affected attribute of an organism would be almost infinite, and a population would consist of a collection of highly disparate individuals in appearance, behavior, and physiology. We should, all of us, be freaks, by comparison with one another. Despite our individual genetic uniqueness, except for monozygotic twins and members of clones and of highly inbred strains, we are relatively minor variants of a modal phenotypic theme that is more narrowly defined by the race or variety representing the pool of unrestricted genetic exchange to which our immediate genealogies may be traced, and more broadly characterized by the subspecies or species to which the narrower taxonomic categories (which exchange genes much more freely within the populations by which they are defined than between them) are genetically allied.

Clearly, the large amount of genetic variability in a population is severely buffered in its very limited phenotypic expression. These modal expressions represent the adaptive phenotypes resulting from the evolutionary history of each taxonomic group (15). The buffering devices include dominance, epistatic interactions, and a variety of limitations on penetrance and expressivity, many of which are now more completely understood as a result of recent findings in physiological and developmental genetics. Population groups may, therefore, share similar phenotypes but differ significantly genotypically. Correlatively, severe phenotypic selection within a noninbred population can produce the appearance of uniformity by means of effects on marker genes and on genes that modify the expression of other genes, while the population remains genetically variable to a degree that cannot be inferred from the range of phenotypic variability exhibited under natural conditions. Such evolved normative phenotypes are, in this sense, highly buffered and can assimilate relatively high amounts of genetic infusion from neighboring populations having somewhat different phenotypic profiles to their own normative phenotypes. This is evidently the case with white and Negro populations in the United States, where the amount of genetic exchange has been estimated to be on the order of 30 per cent (16).

Given the common evolutionary history of the human species, the multiplicity of genetic routes to a phenotypic potential, the assimilation of genetic variability to a comparatively narrow range of phenotypic expression, the relative lack of inbreeding, and the sharing of genes between various human populations both now and in the past, the existence of recognizable subdivisions of the human species that differ from each other genetically and phenotypically cannot be taken to mean that abilities more commonly encountered in one group than in another under present conditions of ascertainment and culture necessarily reflect the true biological differences between the groups under comparison. One does not expect such groups to be genetically or phenotypically identical. Dissimilarities, however, are not in themselves measures of biological fitness. Moreover, under most systems of equal opportunity and equivalent selection, any numerically significant segment of the human species could, by virtue of its genetic variability, probably replace any other with respect to behavioral capacities.

Mating within human population groups is, as previously mentioned, assortative rather than panmictic. Society and culture set the styles in mate selection. Where ethnic groups are differentially treated with respect to the premium that a prevailing culture places on the recognition and nurturing of the full spectrum of their abilities, including economic opportunities which ensure the possessor of certain talents of a chance to identify, develop, and use them, a differential selection system is set up with respect to the partitioning of the gene pool among the groups whose opportunities differ in these respects. Fortunately, this does not create a negative selection in a disadvantaged group. It simply fails to exploit fully the genetic potential available. The democratization of our educational system, the equalization of economic opportunities, and the availability of specialized training to persons possessing special attributes, without regard to racial origin, would be expected to set up assortative mating tracks with respect to such attributes. Even on the extreme assumption that each ethnic group would be reproductively isolated from every other, this way of detecting genetically based abilities and of providing opportunities for persons of comparable endowment to meet and marry would provide for relatively rapid phenotypic equivalence where human abilities are concerned. Social and educational factors are thus viewed as providing tests for the detection of phenotypic variability in behavioral capacities, methods for maximizing the potential of each phenotype, and opportunities for positive phenotypic assortative mating through the selection exerted by colleges, universities, conservatories, art schools, institutes for mechanical training, and many others in which persons of comparable endowment and interest often meet and marry on the basis of these abilities and interests. This has been true of certain segments of the population for a long time. The present social revolution may be expected to apply it even more thoroughly to these segments and to extend it to other segments as well.

There is, therefore, a reciprocity or feedback between the genetic potential of a population and its social structure, such that not only does the former determine what the latter can be, but the latter exerts an important biological effect on the former. It is fortunate that the potential behavioral adaptations do not in any way atrophy from disuse. The deuces remain in the deck, whether the rules of the game are that the deuce is wild or not. While the present assortment of genetic abilities in various population groups may not be numerically equal, they are, in our view, equipotential, and it is our contention that any genetically diverse population existing in reasonable numbers could replace any other on the face of the earth with respect to behavioral abilities, given the prerequisite opportunities for the detection and nurturing of these abilities and for assortative mating to occur on these bases.

REFERENCES

1. Benson E. Ginsburg, "All Mice Are Not Created Equal: Recent Findings on Genes and Behavior," *Social Service Review*, 40 (1966), 121–34.
2. Benson E. Ginsburg, "Genetics as a Tool in the Study of Behavior," *Perspectives in Biology and Medicine*, 1 (1958), 397–424.
3. Benson E. Ginsburg and William S. Laughlin, "The Multiple Bases of Human Adaptability and Achievement: A Species Point of View," *Eugenics Quarterly*, 13 (1966), 240–57.

4. M. L. Watson, "The Inheritance of Epilepsy and Waltzing in *Peromyscus,*" *Contributions from the Laboratory of Vertebrate Genetics* (University of Michigan), No. 11 (1939), 1–24.

5. Governor Witt and Calvin S. Hall, "The Genetics of Audiogenic Seizures in the House Mouse," *Journal of Comparative and Physiological Psychology,* 42 (1949), 58–63.

6. John L. Fuller, Clarice Easler, and Mary E. Smith, "Inheritance of Audiogenic Seizure Susceptibility in the Mouse," *Genetics,* 35 (1950), 622–32.

7. Benson E. Ginsburg and D. S. Miller, "Genetic Factors in Audiogenic Seizures," in *Psychophysiologie, Neuropharmacologie et Biochimie de la Crise Audiogene* (Colloques Internationaux du Centre de la Recherche Scientifique), No. 112 (1963), 217–28.

8. Benson E. Ginsburg, "Causal Mechanisms in Audiogenic Seizures," in *Psychophysiologie, Neuropharmacologie et Biochimie de la Crise Audiogene* (Colloques Internationaux du Centre de la Recherche Scientifique), No. 112 (1936), 229–40.

9. K. Schlesinger, W. Boggan, and D. X. Freedman, "Genetics of Audiogenic Seizures: I. Relation to Brain Serotonin and Norepinephrin in Mice," *Life Sciences,* 4 (1965), 2345–51.

10. Benson E. Ginsburg, "Genetic Parameters in Behavior Research," in Jerry Hirsch, ed., *Behavior-Genetic Analysis* (New York, McGraw-Hill Book Co., 1967)

11. D. G. Freedman, "Constitutional and Environmental Interactions in Rearing of Four Breeds of Dogs," *Science,* 127 (1958), 585–86.

12. William S. Laughlin and Benson E. Ginsburg, "Repackaging People," Kinescope tape, Elizabeth Bailey, producer (University of Wisconsin education television station WHA, 1966).

13. Curt Stern, *Principles of Human Genetics* (2nd ed., San Francisco, W. H. Freeman and Co., 1960).

14. S. Wright, "Statistical Genetics in Relation to Evolution," *Actualités Scientifiques et Industrielles* (Paris, Hermann, 1939).

15. H. C. Bumpus, "The Elimination of the Unfit as Illustrated by the Introduced Sparrow, *Passer domesticus,*" *Biological Lectures Delivered at the Marine Biological Laboratory of Wood's Hole* (Boston, Ginn and Co., 1899).

16. H. Bentley Glass and C. C. Li, "The Dynamics of Racial Intermixture: An Analysis Based on the American Negro," *American Journal of Human Genetics,* 5 (1953), 1–20.

JERRY HIRSCH

Behavior-genetic analysis and the study of man

The justification for my discussion is not so much the novelty of the ideas to be considered (1) as the unfortunate fact that they have so long been *mis*understood. About half a century ago in a most perceptive discussion entitled "The Influence of Darwinism on Philosophy" John Dewey (2) wrote:

> Old ideas give way slowly; for they are more than abstract logical forms and categories. They are habits, predispositions, deeply engrained attitudes of aversion and preference. Moreover, the conviction persists—though history shows it to be a hallucination—that all the questions that the human mind has asked are questions that can be answered in terms of the alternatives that the questions themselves present. But in fact intellectual progress usually occurs through sheer abandonment of questions together with both the alternatives they assume—an abandonment that results from their decreasing vitality and a change of urgent interest. We do not solve them: we get over them. Old questions are solved by disappearing, evaporating, while new questions corresponding to the changed attitude of endeavor and preference take their place.

I shall examine here some of the fallacies that have led to the widespread and long persisting *mis*use of the race concept. It is my intention to show that the notorious nature-nurture or heredity-environment question is, in fact, a pseudo question—a question that is being resolved neither in favor of the position which asserts a racial hierarchy nor of that which asserts absolute biosocial uniformity.

37

More than a century ago, in 1866, J. Langdon H. Down (3)
published a paper in the *London Hospital Reports* entitled "Observations on an Ethnic Classification of Idiots." I know of no better example of the racial hierarchy theory and its misleadingly dangerous implications than his recommendation for

> . . . making a classification of the feeble-minded, by arranging
> them around various ethnic standards—in other words, framing
> a natural system to supplement the information to be derived
> by an inquiry into the history of the case.

> I have been able to find among the large number of idiots
> and imbeciles which comes under my observation, both at Earls-
> wood and the out-patient department of the Hospital, that a
> considerable portion can be fairly referred to one of the great
> divisions of the human family other than the class from which
> they have sprung. Of course, there are numerous representatives
> of the great Caucasian family. Several well-marked examples of
> the Ethiopian variety have come under my notice, presenting
> the characteristic malar bones, the prominent eyes, the puffy
> lips, and retreating chin. The woolly hair has also been present,
> although not always black, nor has the skin acquired pigmentary
> deposit. They have been specimens of white negroes, although
> of European descent.

> Some arrange themselves around the Malay variety, and pre-
> sent in their soft, black, curly hair, their prominent upper jaws
> and capacious mouths, types of the family which people the
> South Sea Islands.

> Nor have there been wanting the analogues of the people who
> with shortened foreheads, prominent cheeks, deep-set eyes, and
> slightly apish nose, originally inhabited the American Continent.

> The great Mongolian family has numerous representatives,
> and it is to this division, I wish, in this paper, to call special
> attention. A very large number of congenital idiots are typical
> Mongols. So marked is this, that when placed side by side, it
> is difficult to believe that the specimens compared are not chil-
> dren of the same parents. The number of idiots who arrange
> themselves around the Mongolian type is so great, and they
> present such a close resemblance to one another in mental power,

that I shall describe an idiot member of this racial division, selected from the large number that have fallen under my observation.

The hair is not black, as in the real Mongol, but of a brownish colour, straight and scanty. The face is flat and broad, and destitute of prominence. The cheeks are roundish, and extended laterally. The eyes are obliquely placed, and the internal canthi more than normally distant from one another. The palpebral fissure is very narrow. The forehead is wrinkled transversely from the constant assistance which the levatores palpebrarum derive from the occipito-frontalis muscle in the opening of the eyes. The lips are large and thick with transverse fissures. The tongue is long, thick, and is much roughened. The nose is small. The skin has a slight dirty yellowish tinge and is deficient in elasticity, giving the appearance of being too large for the body.

The boy's aspect is such that it is difficult to realize that he is the child of Europeans, but so frequently are these characters presented, that there can be no doubt that these ethnic features are the result of degeneration.

And he means degeneration from a higher race to a lower race!

The same pattern of thinking has persisted for 100 years. In the *Encyclopaedia Britannica* (4)—still the best general reference work with which I am familiar—starting with the fourteenth edition in 1929 and appearing repeatedly in all subsequent editions through 1959 [*sic!*], the article on differential psychology describes the inferior intellectual performance of the American Negro as compared with white persons on tests and in the schools. The reader also is informed that "the greater the admixture of white blood, the closer does the Negro approach the white in performance." This discussion was written by a post-World War II president of the American Psychological Association, who was head of the Department of Psychology at Columbia University for many years.

In the foreword to the second edition of Shuey's *The Testing of Negro Intelligence* (5) we are told to let the chips fall where they may:

The honest psychologist, like any true scientist, should have no preconceived racial bias. He should not care which race, if any,

is superior in intelligence, nor should he demand that all races
be potentially equal. He is interested simply in uncovering differences in performance when such exist and in inferring the
origin of these differences.

Hence much of the nonsense asserted about the racial superi-
ority-inferiority pseudo issue by both the egalitarians and the elitists
can be traced to several widely held *mis*conceptions. One misconception
has to do with the statistical properties of trait distributions, and two
others with genotype-phenotype relations and with relations among the
genetic correlates of different phenotypic traits.

First of all, from the Platonistic conception of "general laws" in
theoretical psychology to the "psychic unity of mankind" in cultural
anthropology, a uniformity assumption has survived as a pre-Mendelian,
pre-Darwinian vestige of a typological belief in the fixity of species.
Before Mendel there was no intelligible way of accounting for variation (individual differences)—a problem that gave Darwin no end of
trouble. When the Mendelian mechanism and Darwinian evolution
became part of our intellectual arsenal, however, the uniqueness of
individuals and the evolutionary divergence of the populations they
comprise became immediately comprehensible.

Second, in their striving for objectivity and scientific respecta-
bility, biosocial scientists embraced a Procrustean statistical methodology
which became the *lingua franca* for the description, evaluation, and
discussion of their observations. Unfortunately, it smuggled in a host
of oversimplifying assumptions, which prolonged their commitment to
the already discredited uniformity postulate. The overpopular analysis-
of-variance model, which has been so indiscriminately employed, assumes normality of form and homogeneity of variance in the distributions to be compared (6). Because of those two assumptions, the central tendency of a trait distribution becomes the "typical" value for each
population. All variation around it must be "error." Also, the permissible comparisons between populations are limited to mean values. The
distributions have been arbitrarily assumed to be the same with respect
to all their other properties. Such an approach ignores both the ubiquitous individual differences, which are not error, and the nature of
empirical distributions, so many of which show neither normality nor

homogeneity of variance. Empirically, the invalidity of both assumptions has now been demonstrated many times (7, 8, 9, 10).

Far too many people have found it easy to make the normality assumption needed to satisfy the analysis-of-variance model for two reasons. First, because of the typological uniformity assumption of no individual differences, all variation is considered error and the normal curve provides the most parsimonious way to describe error variation. Second, because the normal distribution is so widely used for evaluating sample statistics, it is *incorrectly* inferred that the populations described by such sample statistics must also be normal. The sampling distribution of a statistic is confused with the trait distribution in the biological population from which the sample was drawn.

Next, although we may pay lip service to the truism that correlation does not mean causation, most of the time we have nothing but correlations with which to work. Our attempts at reductionism—brain and chromosome mapping, for example—and our search for behavioral laws (Platonisms?) have usually been based on an unquestioning and often unrealized acceptance of the counterfactual uniformity postulate—what holds for one individual, the "representative organism," must hold for all. These attempts at reductionism have also been based on a belief that typologically conceived behaviors have a biological basis consisting of *invariably* correlated physical components, which are causally interrelated.

Genetic theory shows very clearly why it is that traits related to the action of *independent* genetic systems can exhibit fortuitous correlations, perhaps indefinitely (11, 12). Many of the trait correlations that distinguish racial, ethnic, and national groups are of just this fortuitous nature. Although they may register statistical significance, they are biosocially unimportant, being maintained by reproductive isolation and our nonrandom, idiosyncratic systems of mating. As Professor Kenneth Mather (13) of England has most aptly remarked:

> Many non-European peoples . . . have been regarded as genetically inferior because their level of social development was below that of the European, and this view has drawn strength from these people's obvious genetical departures from the European in colour and physical characteristics. The existence of

one genetical difference makes it easier to impute another. The falsity of such an argument is self-evident. Since genes can recombine, their effects can be re-associated, so that differences in the genetic determinants of one character do not imply differences in the determinants of another.

I have claimed that the heredity-environment question is a pseudo question to which there is no answer. Let us now examine the reason this is so. In the case of intelligence, the heredity-environment question asks how much of intelligence is due to familial heredity and how much to environmental milieu. The answer usually comes in the form of a heritability estimate—the old familiar nature-nurture ratio, or the per cent due to heredity and the per cent due to environment. The confusion is brought into focus when we ask: Per cents of what are being apportioned to heredity and to environment? The question being asked concerns the ontogeny of a single individual: What is the relative importance of genetic endowment and of environmental milieu in the development of the intelligence of *an* individual? The answers given to that question, however, have nothing to do with *an* individual, nor are they based on the study of development. The answers have been based on the test performance of a cross section of a *population* of individuals at a single time in their lives.

In order to understand the meaning of a measured heritability, it is important to understand how it is obtained. It is derived from the measurement of the expression of some trait by a certain set of genotypes in a certain set of environments. Statistical analysis of such measurements (based on very explicit additivity assumptions) then yields an estimate of the percentage of trait variance that is inferred to be related to the *additive* contemporary genetic variance. Such measurement naturally requires a perfectly balanced experimental design—all genotypes (or their trait-relevant components) measured against all environments (or their trait-relevant components). Few, if any, behavioral studies have been so thorough, and certainly not any human studies.

Only when we consider the number of possible genotypes and the number of potential environments that may influence trait expression do we begin to realize how narrowly limited is the range of applicability for any obtained heritability measure. Twenty years ago J. B. S. Haldane (14) supplied the formula for calculating heredity-environment interactions. For example, if we take 10 genotypes in 10 environments, there are over 7×10^{144} types of interactions. Even for the simplest case but one—2 genotypes in 3 environments or 3 genotypes in 2 environments—there are 60 types of interactions. And by now there is plenty of evidence for the existence of interactions. Therefore, it is ridiculous to attempt to characterize an environment as generally favorable or unfavorable, or any genotype as generally superior or inferior. Some average measure of an environmental influence is applicable *only* to those genotypes affected by it in the same way. Similarly, any rank ordering of genotypes can be applied only in those environments which preserve the ranks of their phenotypes.

It should also be noted that one cannot infer from a high heritability value that the influence of environment is small or unimportant, *as so many people try to do.* When Tryon (15) produced those rats so often mislabeled "bright" and "dull," the difference in their ability to learn his particular maze showed a very high heritability. That does not mean, however, that their maze performance was "genetically determined" in the sense of being developmentally predetermined and unmodifiable. It has since been shown that the use of another training procedure can eliminate the difference between two such strains by raising the level of performance of the so-called dull strain up to that of the so-called bright strain. Therefore, any evaluation of the relative merits of such genotypes depends upon the conditions under which they were observed. Also, the fact that the second training procedure eliminated the difference between the two sets of genotypes provides no basis for inferring what the effects of this training procedure might be for some *other* set of genotypes. All of this means that the characterization of a genotype-environment interaction can only be *ad hoc.* In this context see Mather's (16) account of how the Nobel laureate in physics and professor of engineering science "William B. Shockley . . . falls into one of the classical genetical errors of confusing the apportionment among contributory agencies of the causation of a character itself with the apportionment of causation of the variation it is observed to show."

It was our failure to understand the complexity of the heredity-environment interaction story that encouraged behavioral scientists to believe that they might discover the so-called laws of environmental influence. After all, heredity sets the limits but environment determines the *extent* of development within those limits. Paradoxically that statement is both true and misleading. Its truth lies in its expression of the norm of reaction concept: The phenotypic development of each genotype *is* determined by its ontogenetic environment. [The norm of reaction was beautifully illustrated by Stockard's (17) experiment showing that, when magnesium salts are added to water, eggs of the "normally" two-eyed minnow *Fundulus* develop into an "abnormal" cyclopean form.] The misleading aspects of that statement are due to typological thinking. Because there is no place for individual differences in the typological frame—uniformity is axiomatic—a true statement has been misconstrued as justifying the impossible, that is, the study of environmental influences *per se*. What I call impossible theoretically might at least have been practically feasible (loosely speaking), if the variation pattern for responding to the limitless set of conceivable environmental conditions were exactly the same for all possible genotypes. Since genotypic diversity and genotype-environment interaction are apparently ubiquitous, attempts to study the laws of environmental influence have been grasping at shadows.

The final misconception that I shall consider involves the typological reification of behaviors. The labeling of faculties like intelligence, motivation, anxiety, and the libido may occasionally afford some descriptive convenience. But it becomes positively misleading when it encourages the belief that the same "thing" can always be observed in different species or in different cultures. Just because we can administer the same (operationally defined) test procedure to a pigeon and a rat or to a Harvard student and a Kalahari Bushman does not mean that we are measuring the same behavior—a modern version of what William James called the "psychologist's fallacy."

Several years ago it was shown quite explicitly that, without these fallacious assumptions, there is no "race problem" (18). Races are populations that differ in gene frequencies. On the average, members of one racial population share more ancestors in common with each other than they share with the members of another racial population. Since behavior is a property of organisms, and organisms show surprising variety, there are definite theoretical limitations to the use of organisms for studying some typologically conceived reification called behavior. Behavioral measures, however, are proving to be some of our most sensitive indices of individual and population diversity.

Members of the same species share the same genes. Even though reproductive isolation between populations may be incomplete, the relative frequencies of different alleles of genes in their gene pools are almost certain to differ. Mutations and recombinations may be expected to occur at different places, at different times, and with differing frequencies. Furthermore, selection pressures will also vary (19). Because there are individual differences within populations, because different populations have different gene pools, and because the genetic correlates of most phenotypic traits are mutually independent, there is no reason to expect two populations *ever* to be the same. Therefore, in analyzing distributions of observations (behavioral and other) from different populations we must learn to ask, not whether they are different, but, rather, in what ways they differ. Comparisons must be made with respect to trait distributions, and distributions may differ in any or all parameters—central tendency, dispersion, skewness, kurtosis, etc.

Careful analysis of empirical distributions has already revealed the existence of differences with respect to any one or any combination of parameters. Therefore, no single parameter can any longer be considered exclusively important. That is why we know enough today to expect varying combinations of similarities and differences in the several parameters of distributions when we compare populations with respect to one or more traits, or when we compare traits in one or more populations.

Now, as Dewey suggested, we are learning to ask different questions. Many of us, who once started out to study the genetics *of* behavior, have realized that this is an impossible pursuit. We can study the behavior of *an* organism, the genetics of *a* population, and individual differences in the expression of some behavior by the members of *that* population. For this reason it is less confusing to speak of behavior-genetic analyses, understanding by that expression simultaneously the analysis of well-defined behaviors into their sensory and response components, the reliable and valid measurement of individual differences in the behaviors and in their component responses, and *then* subsequent breeding analysis or, for man, pedigree analysis by the methods of genetics over a specified set of generations in the history of a given population under known ecological conditions. We know very well that both the behavioral and the genetical properties can and will vary over time, over ecological conditions, and among populations. Furthermore, there will be no simple isomorphism between the two.

In the study of man we are learning to ask different questions. It is only when we understand genetics and the complexity of the system of genotype-environment interactions responsible for phenotypes that the problems of genetical analysis and behavioral analysis can be separated rationally. Because of the mosaic nature of the genome, because of mutation, segregation, independent assortment, recombination, and the consequent family transmission pattern for hereditary endowment, we now understand both the ubiquity of individual differences and the importance of their proper study. Before we understood Mendelian genetics, however, the avowed reason for studying individual differences was a hope of relating them to variations in environmental conditions. Because so many genes have pleiotropic effects, because the genetic correlates of so many phenotypic traits are polygenic, because phenocopies do occur, because the norms of reaction are complex, etc., it is now important to separate the problem of inferring the nature of the details of specific genetic systems in man from the study of human phenotypic variation.

We now realize that the description and phenotypic analysis of human variation are legitimate scientific tasks in their own right, and important ones too. Henceforth these tasks must be performed in a manner different from the traditional approach. Instead of random sampling of subjects and the observation of omnibus behaviors like intelligence and personality, we must focus on narrowly defined dimensions of human variation in response, and these will have to be studied in individuals of known biological relationship. The question of the relationships that might prevail for particular phenotypes, between components of their genotype in some population and components of the environment of that population, is a separate, most difficult and complex question.

For all these reasons and for many others, it is now clear that only a biosocial science built upon the most thorough understanding possible of genetics and population structure—a requirement that has remained disgracefully unfulfilled in American psychology, sociology, and anthropology for more than a generation now—only such a science can become free of any preoccupation with the heredity-environment pseudo question.

NOTES AND REFERENCES

1. Some of the ideas considered here have been discussed in Jerry Hirsch, "Intellectual Functioning and the Dimensions of Human Variation," in J. N. Spuhler, ed., *Genetic Diversity and Human Behavior* (Chicago, Aldine Publishing Co., 1967) as well as in the articles in references 8, 11, 12, and 18 below.

2. John Dewey, "The Influence of Darwinism on Philosophy," *Popular Science Monthly* (1909), reprinted in John Dewey, *The Influence of Darwin on Philosophy* (Bloomington, Indiana University Press, 1965), 19.

3. J. Langdon H. Down, "Observations on an Ethnic Classification of Idiots," *London Hospital Reports* (1866), reprinted in Victor A. McKusick, ed., "Medical Genetics 1961," *Journal of Chronic Diseases,* 15 (1962), 432.

4. "Differential Psychology," in *Encyclopaedia Britannica* (editions 1929–1959, Chicago, University of Chicago).

5. Audrey M. Shuey, *The Testing of Negro Intelligence* (2nd ed., New York, Social Science Press, 1966), vii.

6. Churchill Eisenhart, "The Assumptions Underlying the Analysis of Variance," *Biometrics,* 3 (1947), 1–21.

7. R. A. Fisher, F. R. Immer, and Olof Tedin, "The Genetical Interpretation of Statistics of the Third Degree in the Study of Quantitative Inheritance," *Genetics,* 17 (1932), 107–24.

8. Jerry Hirsch, "Genetics of Mental Disease Symposium, 1960: Discussion: The Role of Assumptions in the Analysis and Interpretation of Data," *American Journal of Orthopsychiatry,* 31 (1961), 474–80.

9. J. C. King, "The Fourth Moment of a Characteristic Distribution as an Index of the Regulative Efficiency of the Genetic Code," in R. J. Harris, ed., *Biological Organization at the Cellular and Supercellular Level* (New York, Academic Press, 1963), 129–46.

10. Harry G. Yamaguchi, Clark L. Hull, John M. Felsinger, and Arthur I. Gladstone, "Characteristics of Dispersions Based on the Pooled Momentary Reaction Potentials (S$\overline{E}$R) of a Group," *Psychological Review,* 55 (1948), 216–38.

11. Jerry Hirsch, "Behavior-Genetic, or 'Experimental,' Analysis: The Challenge of Science versus the Lure of Technology," *American Psychologist*, 22 (1967), 118–30.

12. Jerry Hirsch, ed., *Behavior-Genetic Analysis* (New York, McGraw-Hill Book Co., 1967).

13. Kenneth Mather, *Human Diversity: The Nature and Significance of Differences among Men* (New York, The Free Press, 1964), 114.

14. J. B. S. Haldane, "The Interaction of Nature and Nurture," *Annals of Eugenics*, 13 (1946), 197–205.

15. Robert C. Tryon, "Genetic Differences in Maze-Learning Ability in Rats," *Yearbook of the National Society for the Study of Education*, 39 (1940), 111–19.

16. Kenneth Mather, "Genetic Apocalypse?" review of John D. Roslansky, ed., *Genetics and the Future of Man*, in *Nature*, 213 (1967), 126.

17. Charles R. Stockard, "The Artificial Production of a Single Median Cyclopean Eye in the Fish Embryo by Means of Sea Water Solutions and Magnesium Chloride," *Roux' Arch. Entw.-Mech.*, 23 (1907), 249–58.

18. Jerry Hirsch, "Behavior Genetics and Individuality Understood: Behaviorism's Counterfactual Dogma Blinded the Behavioral Sciences to the Significance of Meiosis," *Science*, 142 (1963), 1436–42.

19. Richard H. Post, "Population Differences in Red and Green Color Vision Deficiency: A Review and a Query on Selection Relaxation," *Eugenics Quarterly*, 9 (1962), 131–46.

HERBERT G. BIRCH

Boldness and judgment in behavior genetics

There are excellent reasons for holding a symposium to assess both the state of our knowledge of behavioral genetics and the relevance of this knowledge to one of the major social problems of our country and the world. Such discussion is especially pertinent because of the recent statements by some eminent scientists who, by innuendo or by a scientifically unsophisticated analysis of data fragments, have muddied the water to such a degree that it is increasingly difficult to achieve a scientific approach to the serious problems of social and ethnic inequalities in opportunity, employment, and educational achievement. Making such statements as "the Jukes-Kallikaks 'bad heredity' concept may have been too enthusiastically rejected by perfectionists," raising such questions as "can it be that our humanitarian welfare programs have already selectively emphasized high and irresponsible rates of reproduction to produce a socially relatively unadaptable human strain?" and advancing such meaningless dicta as "heredity controls intelligence more than twice as much as does environment in families that adopt one of a pair of white identical twins" (1) add nothing but noise to our efforts to process available information.

All these statements are from a paper by an American Nobel laureate, William Shockley, and must be disturbing to any serious scientist, not because they reflect an uncongenial set of social attitudes but because they are pseudoscientific nonsense. They revive an outmoded but ever-recurring dichotomy between nature and nurture and fail to profit from the advances in scientific thinking about development which Tobach and Aronson (2), in a review of an equally un-

49

sophisticated book by Lorenz (3), have presented in the following
way: they have indicated and succinctly stated that we must take a
view in which we see all phenotypic expression as "the resultant of
the continuous biochemical and physiological interaction of the gene
complex, cytoplasm, internal milieu and external environment." They
go on to say:

> When a modern geneticist refers to a genetic character, he
> means very specifically that a change in a gene complex pro-
> duces a parallel change in a phenotype. Nowhere does he im-
> ply that genes will enfold into characters without environmen-
> tally and genetically activated maturational processes.

Ginsburg (4), too, expressed this interactive concept, but in a
different way, when he noted that "all aspects of our organism may
be thought of as 100 per cent genetic but not 100 per cent determined."
The confusion between the two concepts "genetic" and "determined"
underlies much of the controversy.

Any contemporary mode of thought concerning behavior and
genetics which fails continuously to appreciate the functional insep-
arability of gene complex and environment in the development of
phenotype is scientifically worthless and reminiscent of the kind of
thinking exhibited by the great biologist and supporter of the abolition
of slavery, T. H. Huxley (5). When confronted with the end of the
American Civil War and the fact of abolition, he said:

> The question is settled; but even those who are most thoroughly
> convinced that the doom is just, must see good grounds for re-
> pudiating half the arguments which have been employed by the
> winning side; and for doubting whether its ultimate results will
> embody the hopes of the victors, though they may more than
> realise the fears of the vanquished. It may be quite true that
> some negroes are better than some white men; but no rational
> man, cognisant of the facts, believes that the average negro is
> the equal, still less the superior, of the average white man. And,
> if this be true, it is simply incredible that, when all his disabili-
> ties are removed, and our prognathous relative has a fair field
> and no favour, as well as no oppressor, he will be able to com-
> pete successfully with his bigger-brained and smaller-jawed rival,

in a contest which is to be carried on by thoughts and not by bites. The highest places in the hierarchy of civilisation will assuredly not be within the reach of our dusky cousins, though it is by no means necessary that they should be restricted to the lowest.

To argue for the necessity of an interactionist view in examining behavior genetics is not to argue that genes are irrelevant to behavior and its development. Dilger (6) has said, "No longer can anyone argue about whether or not the genotype of an animal has an effect on its behavior." However, there is very considerable room to argue about the manner in which this effect is produced. Clearly, the relation is not usually direct but mediated through a series of physiologic and environmental interchanges, which may vary both in kind and in timing with respect to the developmental stage at which they occur. Broadhurst (7) has, as a consequence, pointed out that interactive influences are abundant in any studies of inheritance and behavior and have been insufficiently considered. He said:

> One of the principal difficulties in the investigation of inheritance in any organism is to guard against possible artefacts arising from the influence of the environment. With mammals there is the additional complication of the maternal environment, any possible effect of which must be carefully excluded. Maternal influence can take many forms: what we are concerned with here are what may be termed strain specific, directional effects by which offspring come to resemble parents in respect of the characteristic being studied.

This point should be remembered too from Gross's stimulating series of studies in cancer research (8), which demonstrated very clear transmission of mammary cancer from certain strains of rodent to their female offspring and followed a very interesting sex-linked transmission pattern. Gross found, however, that when he took young of a nontumor strain and gave them to mothers of the tumor strain, the females of these fostered young developed mammary carcinoma at a high rate. This led to a concern about the possibility of viral transmission in milk and other things in the development of mammary carcinoma.

Broadhurst (7) goes on to say:

> These effects are likely to be confused with genetical ones, and
> it is particularly important to exclude them in the study of
> psychological characteristics in the determination of which
> learned and genetically determined effects are frequently con-
> founded. Thus the resemblance of the behaviour of offspring
> to that of the parents may be the result of a common gene pool,
> but it is not permissible to assert that such is the case until
> it has been established that a resemblance is not the result of
> patterns of behaviour having been otherwise transmitted. Much
> of the earlier work in psychogenetics is deficient in this re-
> spect.

A different type of developmental influence is suggested by
King and Shea (9) in their study of subspecific differences in the
responses made by young deer mice to an elevated maze. Considering
clear subspecific differences in behavior, they have argued that

> Usually innate behavioral responses are considered the result of
> some complex physiological reaction or structural difference in
> the nervous system. Another possible interpretation is that the
> differential rates of development in locomotion and the clinging
> response establish rigid patterns of behavior which may endure
> throughout the life of the organism. According to this hypothe-
> sis, *bairdii* become physically capable of locomotion prior to the
> development of a strong clinging response, while *gracilis* de-
> velop their locomotor capacity and clinging tendency simulta-
> neously. Differential rates in morphological development are
> well established. Once falling or the opposite response, clinging,
> is established early in life, it tends to persist throughout the life
> of the mouse.
>
> This characteristic is certainly only one of many other char-
> acteristics which might exhibit differential maturation rates and,
> when interacting with the genetic predisposition of the various
> species and subspecies of *Peromyscus*, might well account for
> the differences in behavior observed throughout this genus.

I think that this kind of analysis of differential rates of underlying physiological maturation or biochemical maturation is pertinent,

too, to an evaluation of the work Dr. Ginsburg reported in this session. Although he thinks he is studying the transmission of susceptibility to sound-induced seizures and does demonstrate strain differences in this trait, he has also demonstrated elsewhere that his animals with sound-induced seizures differ from the ones that do not have such seizures in terms of the rate at which certain transamination processes in the brain develop during the early periods of life. What is being studied phenotypically in behavior, therefore, is not the process that is being directly affected genetically. A similar point is made by Valenstein, Riss, and Young (10), who, in considering genetic and experimental factors in the development of sexual behavior in guinea pigs, indicate that "genetic differences between strains . . . are responsible for differences in the age at which organization of sexual behavior may take place."

It is obvious that these and other differences in rates of maturation and in the patterning of maturation times among separate traits may lead to alterations in the patterns of phenotypic expression, not as a simple genic consequence but because of age-determined differences in the interaction of the organism and his environment. Thus, constancy of phenotype in and of itself is not a sufficient basis for concluding that the *trait*, rather than some morphologic or rate change— often in itself small—affecting the opportunity to develop the trait under given environmental conditions, has been inherited.

This view has economic as well as theoretical significance and is applied at all times when selective breeding procedures have economic meaning and a violation of strict interpretation results in the loss of money. Thus, in considering the relation of genotype to environment for factors of economic significance in poultry, Hull and Gowe (11) warn that

> A stock of animals selected in the past for high performance in some trait cannot be expected to do uniformly well in all environments in which it can be maintained. It is reasonable to assume further that, in some cases at least, optimum performance can only be obtained by selecting distinct strains under the conditions in which they are to be reared.

Consideration of what it is that is most directly produced by a gene complex and a scrupulous reservation in judgment before assuming that gene and phenotype are directly related are of particular im-

portance in considering the central theme of this symposium, the utility
of the construct of race. As it applies to behavior genetics, the construct
has been particularly applied to intellect and has come to be a battle-
ground on which competing social value systems—often uninformed,
yet uniformed in the laboratory smocks of science—have struggled for
a long time and to little avail. In this battle perhaps the most powerful
weapon used by those who wish to argue that differences in intelligence
among races are "inherited" has been the evidence from animal studies
interpreted as demonstrating that learning ability is inherited. The
study most often referred to is the monumental effort by Tryon (12)
to selectively breed animals that learned a maze well and animals that
learned it poorly. In nine generations he was able to produce decidedly
"bright" and "dull" strains. Usually the story stops here and the conclusion is drawn, as by Shockley (1), that "similar rapid changes could
occur for humans." Thus by inference it is implied that this is in fact
what has occurred and that certain "races" have selectively bred so as
to produce people with low intelligence or a gene pool high in poor
learners.

Perhaps the most ubiquitous difficulty in interpreting the data
of behavioral genetics is that the genetics is sometimes sound but almost always the behavioral analysis is terribly poor. What one is given
is the end product of learning in a given maze, or the end score differences in discrimination, or mean differences between groups in
scores on intelligence tests, etc., without any serious effort to determine
what characteristics of the organism as a response system are involved
in the mastery of the presented problems.

I should like to remind those of you who have perhaps forgotten
some phases of the history of animal psychology that this failure to
make a careful study stigmatized whole groups of organisms. For example, when Yerkes (13) studied rats, on the basis of the use of a series
of discrimination box measures, he was able to conclude that a rat's
visual system did not include mechanisms for making discrimination
among shapes and that rats merely could discriminate relative brightness.

It was not until Lashley (14) approached this problem from
the point of view of the hierarchical organization of sense system responsiveness in the rat that this conclusion was shown to be totally
erroneous. Lashley argued that in a given circumstance in which olfac-

tory, tactile, kinesthetic, and visual cues were available, the rat as an organism tended to respond selectively to the nonvisual cues and not to the visual. From these considerations it followed that to determine whether or not the rat had a given organization of visual competence required the elimination or minimization of competing cue systems and the examination of his visual functioning under optimal conditions. Lashley therefore placed his rats upon a very small and narrow jumping stand, and drawing upon his experience in the Alaskan regions, where as a child he had prospected for gold with his father, he caused these animals to jump at windows showing different geometric figures by snapping at them with a miniature dog whip. Under these circumstances, in which a cultural contribution from another region was brought into the psychological laboratory, Lashley was able to demonstrate an exceedingly high order of form discrimination in his rats. Moreover, this served to establish the basis for many psychologists in subsequent generations to earn a livelihood by doing research in discrimination learning.

Fortunately for mankind the usual end of the Tryon "bright" and "dull" rat story is not actually its conclusion but only its middle. The main factual theme that now permits interpretation needs to be stated and the appropriate conclusions drawn from the evidence. To do this is to convert a half-truth, which is always wholly false, into a truth.

It will be remembered that Tryon (12) used an enclosed alley maze as the learning task for separating "bright" from "dull" rats. As the work of Honzik (15), Schneirla (16), Birch and Korn (17), and others suggests, such a task is learned primarily through the use of nonvisual cues. It is possible, therefore, that Tryon was not selectively breeding for "learning ability," "intelligence," "brightness," or "dullness," but for responsiveness to nonvisual cues. Animals that were so selected would work well in his mazes, whereas others, that were more visually responsive, would do poorly when tested on them. This interpretation would lead to a prediction that if the task were changed to one in which responsiveness to visual information would be critical for learning, the results would be reversed, with the formerly "bright" rats being "dull" and the formerly "dull" rats exhibiting a high level of learning ability.

Subsequent evidence produced in a study by Searle (18) entirely supports the preceding interpretation. On a 16-unit elevated maze, in which visual cues are the principal ones used for learning, Searle found the Tryon "dull" rats to be more effective "learners" than the Tryon "bright" strain.

These findings are entirely in accord with the results of Fuller and Thompson (19), who tested five dog breeds on seven behavioral measures, several of which involved learning. On these tests they did, indeed, find differences between breeds, but different breeds appeared to be superior learners on different types of learning tasks. Moreover, the sampling of behavior seemed to them to show "a greater spread between breeds on motivational and emotional characters than on tests involving learning."

These studies and others lead one to question whether the boldness with which implications have been drawn for genetic differences in learning capacity among human groupings from data far less adequate than those available to students of lower mammals does not reflect an absence of sound scientific judgment and a substitution of brashness for thought. If the data of behavioral genetics permit us to draw any conclusions with respect to learning ability it is that learning ability is by no means a unitary trait, and that in different organisms different patterns of responsiveness, of motivation, of emotionality, and of antecedent history contribute substantially to determining which subgrouping will learn most effectively under conditions of different instruction and task demand. It appears, therefore, that a sober judgment would lead us to conclude that differences in learning achievements, whether measured by intelligence tests or by school achievement in human beings, represent the products of different degrees of goodness of fit between the learner, the task, and, in particular, the instructional mode. Such conclusions have positive rather than pejorative implications for a consideration of differences in learning style and achievement in human social groupings.

REFERENCES

1. William Shockley, "Possible Transfer of Metallurgical and Astronomical Approaches to the Problem of Environment versus Ethnic Heredity," unpublished presentation at the Regional Meeting of the National Academy of Sciences, 1966.

2. Ethel Tobach and Lester R. Aronson, review of Konrad Lorenz's *Evolution and Modification of Behavior,* in *Animal Behaviour,* 15 (1967), 201–3.

3. Konrad Lorenz, *Evolution and Modification of Behavior* (Chicago, University of Chicago Press, 1965).

4. Benson E. Ginsburg, "Genetics as a Tool in the Study of Behavior," *Perspectives in Biology and Medicine,* 1 (1958), 397–424.

5. Thomas Henry Huxley, "Emancipation—Black and White [1865]," in *Lectures and Lay Sermons* (New York, E. P. Dutton and Co., 1910), 115–20.

6. William C. Dilger, "The Interaction between Genetic and Experiential Influences in the Development of Species-Typical Behavior," *American Zoologist,* 4 (1964), 155–60.

7. P. L. Broadhurst, "Analysis of Maternal Effects in the Inheritance of Behaviour," *Animal Behaviour,* 9 (1961), 129–41.

8. See Ludwik Gross, "Is Cancer a Communicable Disease?" *Cancer Research,* 4 (1944), 293–303 and "The 'Vertical' Transmission of Mouse Mammary Carcinoma and Chicken Leukemia: Its Possible Implications for Human Pathology," *Cancer,* 4 (1951), 626–33.

9. John A. King and Nancy J. Shea, "Subspecific Differences in the Responses of Young Deermice on an Elevated Maze," *Journal of Heredity,* 50 (1959), 14–18.

10. Elliot S. Valenstein, Walter Riss, and William C. Young, "Experiential and Genetic Factors in the Organization of Sexual Behavior in Male Guinea Pigs," *Journal of Comparative and Physiological Psychology,* 48 (1955), 397–403.

11. P. Hull and R. S. Gowe, "The Importance of Interactions Detected between Genotype and Environmental Factors for Characters of Economic Significance in Poultry," *Genetics,* 47 (1962), 143–59.

12. Robert C. Tryon, "Genetic Differences in Maze-Learning Ability in Rats," *Yearbook of the National Society for the Study of Education,* 39 (1940), 111–19.

13. Robert M. Yerkes and John B. Watson, "Methods of Studying Vision in Animals," *Behavior Monographs,* 1 (1911), 1–90.

14. K. S. Lashley, "The Mechanism of Vision: 1. A Method for Rapid Analysis of Pattern-Vision in the Rat," *Journal of Genetic Psychology,* 37 (1930), 353–460.

15. C. H. Honzik, "Cerebral Control in the Maze Learning of Rats," *Journal of Comparative Psychology,* 15 (1933), 95–132.

16. T. C. Schneirla, "Learning and Orientation in Ants," *Comparative Psychology Monographs,* 6 (1929), 1–143.

17. Herbert G. Birch and Sam J. Korn, "Place-learning, Cognitive Maps, and Parsimony," *Journal of General Psychology*, 58 (1958), 17–35.
18. L. V. Searle, "The Organization of Hereditary Maze-Brightness and Maze-Dullness," *Genetic Psychology Monographs*, 39 (1949), 279–325.
19. John L. Fuller and W. Robert Thompson, *Behavior Genetics* (New York, John Wiley and Sons, 1960).

J. P. SCOTT

Discussion

RACE AS A CONCEPT

From a biological viewpoint the term race has become so encumbered with superfluous and contradictory meanings, erroneous concepts, and emotional reactions that it has almost completely lost its utility. Any scientist who continues to use it will run a major risk of being misunderstood, even if he rigorously limits his own definition. He will run the additional risk in his own thinking of finding it difficult to avoid past misconceptions.

The term should therefore be replaced with the concept of the population. The latter is a neutral term with few connotations and has in recent years proved useful in investigating the biological realities of breeding structure, gene pools, and gene flow. It is to be hoped that the understanding of the biological nature of populations will eventually lead to the abandonment of the term race, with its undesirable and erroneous connotations. As this happens the result will be a scientific revolution, one which is already having a slow but inevitable world-wide effect on human social behavior and organization.

From the viewpoint of the social sciences, the concept of race is a set of beliefs shared by many human beings and is thus a sociological phenomenon which, together with its behavioral consequences, forms a legitimate field of scientific study. The fact that many of these beliefs are based on typological thinking and erroneous information does not immediately affect their existence, although it may do so in the long run. In short, what people believe affects their behavior, whether their beliefs are true or not. Scientists should therefore be unusually careful to stick to scientifically established facts and to avoid speculation in any public discussion of this phenomenon.

59

RELEVANCE OF RESULTS OBTAINED FROM INFRAHUMAN ANIMALS TO HUMAN BEHAVIOR

People often look to animals to justify human activities. A notable example in the nineteenth century was Social Darwinism, which used the phenomenon of natural selection in animal populations to justify certain sharp business practices common in the early part of the industrial revolution in England and America. In the same era, other individuals pointed to examples of monogamous mating in animals in order to justify our particular form of marriage. In a similar way, one can find animal examples of almost any sort of human social practice or belief and, by avoiding the contradictory instances, make a case for almost any type of human behavior, no matter how noble or debased it may be from an ethical standpoint.

Needless to say, such justifications are fundamentally unsound. From a strict scientific viewpoint, the human species is genetically unique, and one cannot apply any conclusion derived from another species directly to our own. The final test of any theory derived from other animals must be made on the human species itself.

Infrahuman animal populations are similar to human populations only in ways in which they can be directly demonstrated to be similar, or have been deliberately made similar, as in the case of some of the domestic animals. The human species is a unique population in the degree to which it is spread all over the land surface of the globe (possibly excluding Antarctica), encompassing all sorts of climates and ecological conditions. The only species which share this world-wide distribution are certain of man's parasites and one of his domestic animals, the dog.

The dog is therefore an attractive species to compare with human populations. But this must be done in a realistic way, always remembering that the dog has an entirely different genetic base. The various breeds, as now managed by dog clubs and breeders' associations, are populations which for the most part are kept separate from each other. They are not, however, equivalent to human populations occupying different geographic areas, but more closely resemble the caste systems which are still enforced in some human populations. As populations selected by breeders for particular morphological and behavioral traits, they are not equivalent to any human populations, since deliberate selection has never been practiced among human beings. If dogs do form a model for human populations, it is as a parallel case of extreme variation between individuals—that is, the differences between dog breeds are comparable in magnitude to those between individuals in a large human population.

THE IMPLICATIONS OF ANIMAL BEHAVIOR AND BEHAVIOR GENETICS

Although a beginning has been made on the study of human behavior genetics (1), chiefly using the twin method, most work so far has been done on lower animals. Keeping in mind that direct application of ideas derived from other species is unjustified, we can suggest the following hypotheses for testing in human populations.

Antagonism between like individuals

Studies of fighting among different species of birds indicate that a male bird defending its territory or a bird competing for food at a feeding station is most likely to attack a member of its own species, next most likely to attack a member of a closely related species, and least likely to attack a member of a distantly related species (2). An experiment by King (3) indicated that when strange dogs were introduced into a naturally formed group, most antagonism was directed toward individuals of the same sex and similar breed, and least antagonism toward members of the opposite sex and different breed. The implication here is that there is no "natural antagonism" between unlike individuals, and the question may be raised whether this is also true of human beings. At the very least, there is no justification for the common belief that antagonism between unlike human beings is a "natural" phenomenon shared by other animals.

Limited relationship between physical characteristics and behavior

The results of our extensive studies (4) on the correlation between physical characteristics and behavior in dogs can be summarized as follows:

1. Such superficial characteristics as hair color and hair length have no relation to behavior other than obvious secondary effects; for example, a short-haired dog seldom sits long on a cold surface. In another case, the homozygous condition of the dominant merle gene produces all-white animals that are partially blind and deaf, and their behavior is affected secondarily by these sensory deficiencies.

2. Physical measurements such as height, weight, and chest circumference show only low correlations with behavior, and show these most often in purebred animals. The inference is that differences in physique produce consistent effects only among genotypically similar individuals.

The evidence from our experiments is therefore against the notion that important behavioral differences are associated with superficial appearance. This conclusion has most significance for dog breeders, but it also lends no support to the idea that superficial differences in skin color and hair form are associated with genetically determined differences in human behavior.

Evolution toward adaptation

Among long-lived animals such as mammals, living in environments which continually fluctuate, there has been evolution, not toward fixed patterns of adaptive behavior, but toward the ability to change and vary behavior. In addition, there has been evolution toward increasing ability to modify behavior as a result of previous experience. In short, while there are certain species of mammals which are relatively undeveloped in these respects, the most successful are those whose behavior is marked by adaptability and the capacity to learn.

These are extremely unspecialized abilities. However, when we investigate behavioral differences between different breeds of dogs, we find evidence, not of general differences in adaptive capacities, but rather of differences of a highly specialized sort (4). This evidence, such as it is, is against major differences in general intelligence between populations within a species. Because of the difficulty of compensating for cultural differences it may never be possible to answer this question fully with respect to human populations, but the animal evidence indicates that if differences exist, they are most likely to be of a special nature. Furthermore, our experiments with dogs showed that even with a large amount of deliberate selection, which has not occurred in human populations, there is still a great deal of overlap among individuals belonging to different breeds. One would therefore predict that between large human populations there would be only rather small average differences and that these would be related to special rather than general abilities.

Genetic homeostasis

The experiments of Lerner (5) and others with attempts to modify physiological characteristics of animal populations resulted in the discovery that genetic systems appear to be buffered against the effects of selection. A typical result is that changes in a population under selection proceed rather rapidly for five or six generations and then come to a standstill. If selection is relaxed, the population drops back toward its former condition.

Studies by Erlenmeyer-Kimling, Hirsch, and Weiss (6) and Dobzhansky and Spassky (7) on selection for behavioral differences in *Drosophila* have given similar results. In addition, there is a simple genetic model that would explain these effects.

Tryon's (8) experiment with crossing rats selected for differences in maze-learning ability produced the unusual genetic result of an F_1 as variable as the F_2 and covering the range of both parent populations, although the F_1 generation should theoretically consist of one genotype. This result has turned up several times in behavior genetics experiments, and in at least two instances in our work with breed crosses in dogs (4). There are several possible explanations, depending on the circumstances of the experiment, but one that fits our dog data is that the F_1 generation, consisting of heterozygous individuals, is located near a threshold of response, with the result that random environmental factors determine whether or not these animals respond to stimulation and thus fall into one parental class or the other. The result of such a genetic system would be a population that could change very rapidly under conditions of selection favoring one response or the other, although it would be very resistant to the establishment of a completely pure strain. We can therefore suggest the hypothesis that a population which has such genetic systems is better adapted for survival than one which is not buffered against the effects of selection.

Applied to human populations, this would suggest that populations which might behave quite differently under different conditions of physical environment or culture, and in which selection might be presumed to be taking place, might actually resemble each other quite closely under similar environmental conditions. In short, as soon as the selection pressures which kept the two populations apart were relaxed, they would tend to revert to a greater degree of similarity.

The importance of emotional and motivational differences

Experiments with both direct selection and with breed differences established by previous selection emphasize the importance of emotional and motivational factors affecting behavioral performance. There appears to be a great deal of genetic variance in such characteristics in animal populations. Whether or not an animal is fearful of strange objects has a strong effect on his performance when unfamiliar pieces of apparatus are used, and in a problem-solving situation involving food rewards, animals that are strongly motivated by food obviously try harder and are more likely to achieve success. The effects of such factors as these are compounded by the principle of success motivation, namely, that if behavior is rewarded or reinforced, it becomes strengthened. Relatively small genetic differences can be magnified in this way by training and experience.

The implication is that if we wish to find genetic variation in important characteristics affecting behavior in human populations, we should begin to look for emotional and motivational differences rather than for differences in performance. The latter are so radically modified by culture and previous experience that genetic comparisons between populations are almost impossible. Whether or not emotional and motivational differences do exist between human populations is a completely open question, and one can predict only that individual variation along these lines is quite likely to be found.

Lack of direct relationship between gene and behavior

It is a truism that behavior cannot be biologically inherited but must be developed and elicited under the combined influence of genetic and environmental factors. The effects of genes must be expressed through physiological action, and it has long been known that genes modify each other's effects so that only when a gene has a major and usually disruptive effect is there a one-to-one relationship between gene and character. The effect of a gene, therefore, depends upon the particular gene combination in which it is found, and in any large variable population there are inevitably an almost infinite number of such combinations.

In addition, genetic effects on behavior are modified by behavioral adaptation. When confronted with a problem, an animal will try out various solutions and adopt one that seems to be successful. Most practical problems can be solved by using a variety of combinations of capacities, with the result that the same end result can be achieved by a number of different genetic varieties of individuals.

What this means, of course, is that two populations may appear to be behaviorally identical even though they are known to be genetically different, and behaviorally different under slightly different environmental conditions even if genetically identical. The range of human adaptation is so great that it is doubtful whether population differences on any behavioral test of complex performance ever can be assigned to any definite genetic basis. It also means that, when necessary, human beings should be able to do the same things and thus adapt to each other, no matter what their background of individual or population differences.

GENETIC CONSEQUENCES OF THE NATURE OF HUMAN POPULATIONS

From the genetic viewpoint, a population may be defined as a group of individuals whose members interbreed. Present-day human populations defined in this way are for the most part extremely large, and there is an increasing tendency for them to coalesce. In addition, human populations show a lengthy span between generations, amounting to twenty-five years on the average, and with very rare exceptions, individuals have few offspring. The result is that human populations are extremely stable from a genetic viewpoint and that genetic changes under modern conditions are extremely slow. Furthermore, in modern times there have been very few instances in which a population has been completely wiped out, with the result that the possibility of selection between populations is very small and any changes produced in this way are even slower.

In contrast, there is every indication from historical and anthropological sources that cultural change has been taking place with considerable rapidity in historical time, and that the tempo of change is increasing. From the results with infrahuman animals, one would expect that four or five generations, amounting to a century or more, would be required before any considerable effect of selection would be noticed in a human population. On the other hand, great cultural changes have taken place in the past half-century. If such changes continue in the future, there should be no consistent genetic effect of cultural selection on human behavior. Furthermore, there is a tendency for cultures to become more similar as the interchange of information increases, with the result that random changes produced by cultural selection should have a smaller and smaller effect in producing population differences.

GENETICS AND SOCIAL ORGANIZATION

Most theoretical studies of population genetics have assumed infinite size and random mating. The former assumption is very nearly true of many human populations, but the latter is not, and in fact is not true of any infrahuman animal population with even a moderately high degree of social organization. The individuals accessible for mating are determined by geographical proximity, dominance organization, and patterns of sexual behavior. The information necessary to define the mating structure of an animal population is not available in most cases and will not be until studies with identified individuals are made over long periods of time. Social selection may be involved in both the choice of mates and the differential survival of offspring.

In human populations there are cultural differences in mating patterns that should produce widely different genetic results. An example is the contrast between a small primitive tribe divided into clans with a rule of exogamy and a large industrial society like our own, combining a great deal of geographic mobility with a taboo against incest.

One of the consequences of modern economic organization and division of labor is that individuals having the same occupation are likely to be thrown into contact with each other and hence are more likely to marry. Such assortative mating may have some genetic consequences, but since individuals performing the same sorts of tasks with the same degree of skill may have widely different combinations of genes, it is not likely to produce a genetic caste system, but rather to introduce new and unusual combinations of genes. As Dobzhansky has pointed out, this may result in individuals with unusual abilities, but not necessarily in a class of genetically similar individuals.

SUMMARY

To summarize, it is almost a truism that what people do is more important than what they are, and that the details of their physique and structure are important only in terms of how these affect behavior. Differences in behavior can be studied on two levels: the differences between individuals, and the differences between populations. Behavior-genetics studies in lower animals indicate that there is much variation between individuals in the same population, even in populations, like those of the dog breeds, that have been subjected to a great deal of selection for uniformity. The dog breeds themselves are not comparable to human populations but, if anything, provide information regarding the degree of individual variation that is possible within a highly social species holding a dominant ecological position and relieved from many sorts of selection pressures.

Behavior-genetics studies on animals indicate that more attention should be paid to genetic differences in emotional and physiological factors rather than to tests of performance. Although modifiable by training, genetic differences are less subject to reorganization and are thus more directly related to primary gene action, and have clear-cut effects on performance. While the concept of race is a sociological fact and should be studied in this context as long as people believe in race, it should, from the genetic viewpoint, be replaced by that of populations, gene pools, and gene flow. With these concepts, we can make useful advances toward greater knowledge of the human species and at the same time accelerate the process of bringing about a scientific revolution in some of the ideological concepts that affect social behavior and organization.

REFERENCES

1. Steven G. Vandenberg, *Methods and Goals in Human Behavior Genetics* (New York, Academic Press, 1965).

2. J. Fisher, "Interspecific Aggression," in J. D. Carthy and F. J. Ebling, eds., *The Natural History of Aggression* (New York, Academic Press, 1964).

3. John A. King, "Closed Social Groups among Domestic Dogs," *Proceedings of the American Philosophical Society*, 98 (1954), 327–36.

4. J. P. Scott and J. L. Fuller, *Genetics and the Social Behavior of the Dog* (Chicago, University of Chicago Press, 1965).

5. I. M. Lerner, *Genetic Homeostasis* (London, Oliver and Boyd, 1954).

6. L. Erlenmeyer-Kimling, Jerry Hirsch, and Jane M. Weiss, "Selection and Hybridization Analyses of Individual Differences in the Sign of Geotaxis," *Journal of Comparative and Physiological Psychology*, 55 (1962), 722–31.

7. Theodosius Dobzhansky and Boris Spassky, "Selection for Geotaxis in Monomorphic and Polymorphic Populations of *Drosophila Pseudoobscura*," *Proceedings of the National Academy of Sciences*, 48 (1962), 1704–12.

8. Robert C. Tryon, "Genetic Differences in Maze-Learning Ability in Rats," *Yearbook of the National Society for the Study of Education*, 39 (1940), 111–19.

EDMUND W GORDON

Discussion

In the four formal presentations at this session the question of the utility of the construct "race" has been approached more or less obliquely and in a number of ways. Kilham and Klopfer presented data which support the position that in a given animal strain perceptual systems—and probably other behavioral systems—are so organized that particular prerequisite experiences are required for certain responses to become possible and are so programmed that potential responses to certain kinds of behavior are limited. Their work suggests that a particular experiential prerequisite and the related response potential are characteristics of a particular strain of organism. Obviously, their work supports the fact that subgroup differences exist in species of animals. If one chooses to assign a collective or racial label to subgroups which can be identified by some common pattern of characteristics, there can be no argument that the construct "race" cannot be ignored since taxa below the level of the species are a fact of nature.

In their concern with the multiple bases of human adaptability and achievement, Ginsburg and Laughlin take as granted the fact of differential genetic patterning between subgroups of the human species, but go on to make the case for the existence within the various subgroups of adequate genetic diversity and adaptive potential "to replace the entire human species with genotypically well-adapted populations." For their purposes the existence of subgroup or racial differences is less important than the existence of genetic potentials or pools which make for wide variations in adaptation and genetic restructuring, while retaining an essential genetic unity. They are thus as much concerned with the factors which make for the genetic unity of the species as with expressions of genetic variation or difference within

69

the species. For the former, the construct "race" seems to have little utility save for classification of subgroups, in the latter, "race" seems to be significant primarily for purposes of identification and comparison. It is their plea for comparative studies, conducted by multidisciplinary teams, under conditions which respect the context in which the target characteristics have developed and are observed, which I choose to underscore and support. If the construct "race" can contribute to fostering such research without supporting our typical underestimation and underreporting the characteristics of groups accorded lower status, it can have utility.

Hirsch correctly rejects, as do Ginsburg and Laughlin, the use of the construct "race" to assert a genetically based hierarchical relationship between subgroups of the human species. Rather, specific characteristics by which subgroups can be identified must be viewed in the context of the circumstances under which they have developed and in relation to their adaptive relevance to the demands of the indigenous environment. All constellations of human characteristics are not equally adaptive for all environmental circumstances, so that when a particular set of environmental conditions is taken as the norm against which potential for meeting adaptive demands is judged, subgroups can be arranged hierarchically. But as environmental conditions change, the nature of adaptive requirements may also shift, making for changes in the value we assign to specific potentials for adaptation. We do not place a high value on race horses where the social need is for pack horses.

Hirsch has also placed the old "nature-nurture" controversy in a more appropriate context. Just as the value assigned to a particular behavioral characteristic is largely determined by the circumstances under which it is called into play, the nature and form in which the characteristic emerges are not predetermined and fixed but are products of a genotype-environment interaction. Having been preoccupied with "either/or" and "how much of which" strategies, we know little of this interaction. Hirsch bids us study it through the separate but related processes of behavioral and genetical analyses.

My colleague, mentor, and friend, Herbert Birch, has none too delicately placed the question of the utility of the construct "race" in still another context. He has no special difficulty with the term but is grossly intolerant of most of the interpretations which have been made of data referable to race. Like Hirsch, he feels that incorrectly posed questions around the "nature-nurture" issue seriously distort the judgment of workers in this field, chiefly because they confuse two concepts, "genetic" and "determined." In the study of human behavior the two terms apply but not in a static and invariant manner; all behavior is genetically based but not solely genetically determined. Birch concludes that in some features of the development of intellective behavior, differences in learning achievements represent different degrees of goodness of fit between the learner, the task, and the instructional mode. In comparative studies of racial or ethnic groups, however, the concern too often has been with gross measures of intellectual achievement, as if learning ability were a unitary trait, manifested in a single style, and unvaried in its expression under different conditions of stimulation and response. In referring to instructional mode and learning ability, Birch introduced into this symposium a bridge between the concern with and reference to animal research and the teaching-learning process in human subjects, which is the prime concern of my own work.

As an educational psychologist concerned with understanding the mechanisms by which patterned behaviors emerge, are directed, and may be modified, I find that the construct "race" has little or no utility. This is not to argue that race as a construct has no validity. I readily acknowledge the existence of differences in structure and behavior potentials that may be functions of reasonably stable genetic patterning and that these differences can and do emerge as dominant in or characteristic of a particular animal strain, stock, or race. The question is not whether animal groups with common characteristics exist or whether there are differences between groups of animals classified according to certain common characteristics. We must consider higher level questions: What is the relevance of such classification to understanding the mechanisms of behavioral development? And more important, what is the relevance of specific characteristics or behavior potentials to the emergence, guided development, and modification of patterned behavioral development and learning?

Historically, human societies have not had the privilege of being concerned with the universal optimal development of their members. Governed largely by economic scarcity, greater attention was given to selecting those members most likely to succeed or those whose station in life "entitled" them to the opportunity. Under such a system, the rather static concern with identification and classification was appropriate to the limitations inherent in those stages of societal development. Given such circumstances, the construct "race" and the distortions in its use are at least understandable; it may even be said that for such out-dated social systems, the construct "race" had some utility. Through its use one could quickly identify those members from whom little would be expected and for whom little would be done.

As more and more societies have reached a point in development where material resources are sufficient to move from favoring those most likely to succeed toward ensuring that all will have adequate opportunity to succeed, and as these societies reach the stage of technological development where it is essential that all members reach optimal levels of achievement, the major focus can no longer be on prediction and selection. Prime attention must be given to directed behavioral development and modification. In fulfilling the important task of advancing the development of behavior in man in today's complex societies, race studies serve little useful purpose, but behavior and genetic analyses directed at understanding and guiding the behavior of individuals and groups are of crucial importance.

A principal function of education is to guide the development of behavior; yet education has been dominated by the views that behavioral development is predetermined and greatly limited by heredity and that behavior potentials are at least significantly influenced by race. The impact of these views on education is reflected in the following conditions, which are found frequently in the educational enterprise:

1. A laissez-faire or neglectful attitude toward the training and development of intelligence;
2. A monitoring as opposed to a stimulating approach to academic and social readiness and personality development;
3. An exaggerated emphasis on the predictive value of classification and quantification of psychological appraisal data and a neglect of qualitative appraisal data as a basis for planning and intervention;
4. Distortion of aspiration and expectation levels based upon unjustified ceilings on potentials for human development and adaptation;
5. Placement of the burden of proof (a) on the examinee rather

than on the appraiser or appraisal method; (*b*) on the learner rather than on the teacher or teaching method; and (*c*) on the counselee rather than on the counselor or counseling method;

6. Emphasis on adjustment or acceptance of assumed realities rather than on modification of the environment and the individual's interaction with it;

7. Overemphasis on selection and placement (educational and vocational) and underemphasis on the nurturing of interests and aptitudes and the development and training of capacities and skills; and

8. An eclectic and empirical approach to research in directed learning with little application of the scientific method in exploration, experimentation, and investigation.

In no aspect of the educational enterprise are these influences more deleterious than in our current efforts at improving education for disadvantaged populations by utilizing a wide variety of traditional educational practices. In a nationwide review of special programs and practices designed for such persons, one is impressed by the magnitude of this effort. However, it is distressing to note that few of these endeavors have made significant changes in the functioning of the pupils toward whom they are directed. One could argue that there is little payoff in these programs because the pupils are of limited potential. An alternative argument is that the programs do not constitute an appropriate match between learner characteristics, learning tasks and learning experiences. Consequently, they do not result in significant improvements in pupil performance. We do not have the empirically derived data to give definitive support to either of these positions; however, they are the kinds of questions which grow out of the controversial issues underlying this symposium. We can argue these issues forever, but their solution will come only from serious research. It is hopeful that we are at least asking questions rather than advancing positions polemically. In the final analysis, though, we are left with the crucial question of how man influences the quality and content of the behavioral repertoire. Two years ago I concluded an article with this statement:

To honor our commitments to science and professional service, we must understand the limitations of our knowledge and our practice. Much of what we do is based on the hopeful assumption that all human beings with normal neurological endowment can be developed for participation in the mainstream of our society. We believe this because we have seen many people from a great variety of backgrounds participate and because we want to believe it. But we do not yet have definite evidence to support our belief. We operate out of an egalitarian faith without knowing whether our goals are really achievable. Yet it must be our aim, not only as scientists and professional workers, but as humanitarians as well, to determine the potential of human beings for equality of achievement.* If in the light of our most sophisticated and subtle evaluations, we conclude that such equality is not generally achievable, if in spite of the best we can do it seems likely that some of our citizens will remain differentiated by their own biology, then we shall merely have answered a persistent question. We will still have no evidence that group differences per se imply any inability on the part of particular individuals to meet the demands of society. We will then be able to turn our energies to helping individuals meet those demands. And if, on the other hand, as we believe, true equality of opportunity and appropriate learning experiences will result in equality of achievement, then we must so organize our professional services and our society that no person is kept from achieving that potential by our indifference to his condition, by the inadequacy or inappropriateness of our service, or by the impediments society deliberately or accidentally places in his path. It is not an unhopeful paradox that the only way we shall ever know whether equality of human achievement is possible is through providing for all our citizens, privileged and underprivileged, the kind of service and society that assumes it is possible and makes adequate provision for the same.

---

* The term equality of achievement is used with an unspecified subgroup reference and is not intended to violate or ignore what is known concerning individual differences.

TWO ❖ BIOLOGICAL ASPECTS OF RACE IN MAN

THEODOSIUS DOBZHANSKY

Introduction

Science aims to help man understand himself and his place in the universe. Yet man's efforts to know himself are often frustrated by his propensity to deceive himself. This propensity reaches its pinnacle where so-called sensitive topics are involved. The topic of race is one of these; it elicits emotional, and often passionate, reactions in many people.

Faced with this situation, what posture should a scientist adopt? Two extreme attitudes, opposite in sign, are equally unfortunate. One is to leave the whole problem in abeyance, because of the risk that scientific findings may be misinterpreted and misused. The other is to adopt a make-believe detachment, pretending that scientists need not be concerned about the uses and misuses of their discoveries. Both attitudes betray irresponsibility. Science is not a collection of random facts, however accurately observed. It is a human endeavor to sort out the significant from the trivial. The world in which we live is hungry for simple solutions to complex problems; complex problems may not have simple solutions, but they ought to have at least comprehensible ones.

In biology and anthropology the concept, or construct, of race has two aspects. Race is a category of classification; it is also a biological phenomenon. This duality has profound philosophical and methodological roots. Classification is a necessity. Bronowski wrote that science is "the search to discover unity in the wild variety of nature—or, more exactly, in the variety of our experience." Language is the oldest instrument for coping with this wild variety. By giving names to things, man reduces the variety to manageable proportions. There are more than three billion persons in the world today, and nobody can know them all individually; it is necessary to group, to classify, to name them. If races did not exist they would have to be invented. Since they do exist they need not be invented, they need to be understood.

Some people have claimed that nothing new has been discovered for a long time about human races or about races in general. I hope that this symposium will show how far off the mark is this claim. In this introduction I can indicate only the general direction of the newer race studies. The inhabitants of different parts of the world are often visibly different, and the differences are in part genetic. This, in a nutshell, is the essence of race as a biological phenomenon. To be sure, any two persons, even brothers and sisters, also differ. Race differences are genetic differences between Mendelian populations, not between persons. And yet races differ in the same traits in which persons also differ. Difficulties arise because when a race or any other group is given a name, one is likely to assume that the individuals composing the group are alike or at least very similar. This is typological thinking, which befuddles not only the man in the street but some scientists as well. Professor Mayr has quite rightly pointed out that the most important reform in biological conceptualization in recent years has been the abandonment of typological misconceptions.

Race differences are compounds of individual differences; they are more often relative than absolute; races differ in the frequencies of some genes more often than in that a certain gene is wholly absent in one race and present in every individual of another. This relativity, the lack of hard and fast dichotomies in race differences, is disappointing to the adherents of the old-fashioned typological concept of races. Curiously enough, it is also disappointing to some new-fashioned writers, who claim that since races are not airtight pigeonholes they do not exist at all. They say that the human species, mankind, has no races. I think that this is the same old typological misconception turned inside out. If man has no races, where are races to be found? And if they are nowhere found, why then are the inhabitants of different countries often recognizably different? One may or may not accept this "no-race" hypothesis, but the very fact that it has been seriously advocated shows that the race concept is far from being a self-evident cliché. It is an open problem that needs further study.

In this section we will consider the biological, rather than the sociological, aspects of race. There is, however, one point that must be made clear at the outset. Except for identical twins, everybody is biologically, genetically, different from everybody else. Diversity should not, however, be confused with inequality. Equality and inequality are sociological, and identity and diversity are biological phenomena. Diversity is an observable fact; equality, an ethical precept. Society may grant or withhold equality from its members; it could not make them genetically alike even if this were desirable.

LOREN EISELEY

Race: the reflections of a biological historian

Thirty years have passed since, as a graduate student, I first visited the nation's capital. I had driven down from the University of Pennsylvania in the company of Oriental friends from four Far Eastern nations. Those were the years of the depression—not of grants—and each of the young men who accompanied me had come from a family of wealth and cultivation across the Pacific. What I experienced on that afternoon and evening has left a lifelong impression upon my mind. It has taught me also that under sufficient external pressure one's group identification can alter. I was for some weeks thereafter an interior Oriental, and so traumatic was the experience to which I was subjected that I have never been quite sure of my racial identification since.

The episode began quite innocently with a delay in repairs upon our car that seemed to make it advisable to spend the night in Washington. At hotels, even at certain Christian hostelries which I shall not mention, we were turned away. Always all rooms seemed to be filled just as we crossed the threshold. Finally we turned wearily to seeking lodging in the suburbs where, in that time, the motor tourist could find accommodation. After several rejections I made one last try. A pinch-faced, irascible landlady appeared. At first negotiations seemed to be going well. Then she gestured toward the Japanese lad behind me. "Is this your man?" she queried.

"No," I said with stupid honesty. "He is my friend." The crash of the door shutting in my face almost broke the glass.

We turned silently to the car and just as silently started the long night's journey back to Philadelphia. We were leaving a great world capital still dominated by an insular slave tradition and a color bar so rigid that a white man who stepped over it was cast beyond the pale as completely as if his skin color had undergone a sudden mutation. And so mine had, in a figurative sense at least. Safe home in the Chinese restaurant frequented by my friends, I resumed the use of chopsticks among people to whom I felt far more akin than to those who were willing to house a member of another race only so long as it was clear that he was "my man" but not my friend and social equal. The episode was an all-too-evident indication of the staying power of traditional mores, whatever the world of science might choose to enunciate upon the subject of race.

I mention this painful incident, not to lacerate my feelings with old memories or to forgo proper scientific objectivity, but rather to emphasize at the outset of my remarks that however calmly we may discourse upon the subject of race in the laboratory or classroom, we find that in the end it escapes into the street and assumes multiple guises which have little to do with gene percentiles, clines, or biological immunities. I applaud the research that has gone into these endeavors. By slow seepage into the body politic such knowledge may erode prejudice. Yet thirty years ago that knowledge was largely available, and over three hundred years previously one of the first great spokesmen of science, Francis Bacon, had stated, in essence, the scientific position which we assume today; namely, that it is primarily social heredity and not biological endowment which makes for striking cultural distinctions among races. "Man," Bacon said, speaking of the savages of the New World, "[may be] a god to man. And this difference," he continues in the Novum Organum, "comes not from the soil, not from race, but from the arts"—that is, in modern terms, culture. Lest the truth of that observation be still obscured, let us remember that five thousand years ago barbaric Europeans, the forefathers of many of us, squatted on shell heaps around the Baltic while civilization was stirring on the shores of the Mediterranean. I am sure that to the southern people of our race in Europe we spoke then in barbarous and illiterate tongues and were scarcely deemed civilizable. For generations we chipped stone daggers in humble imitation of the metal weapons that we did not possess.

Between Bacon's observation and our own stretch three centuries of experience of the world, centuries of far voyaging and of contact with unknown peoples in peace and war. It is the age of the new science. Through all that time biology and evolving social thought have grappled with the problem of race. To review briefly the meanderings of that thought is to see at once that the institution of science itself cannot be totally detached from the political and economic atmosphere in which it flourishes. How much more attractive, therefore, must have proved those racial preconceptions which furthered already existing systems of belief.

There was the involvement of race in a changing Christian theology; there was the growing recognition of the enormous relativity of culture and, in spite of Bacon's warnings, its confusion with doctrines of biological superiority and inferiority. There were the changed conceptions of race that came in with evolution and the recognition of natural selection. There is the way in which Darwinism itself, and through it science, unwittingly promoted prejudice, as when Darwin wrote, somewhat ethnocentrically and awkwardly in *The Descent of Man,* "With civilised nations . . . the increased size of the brain from greater intellectual activity, [has] . . . produced a considerable effect on their general appearance when compared with savages" (1). Other Victorians, far less cautious than Darwin, made free with the conception of the non-Caucasoid races as living fossils.

That this conception bears a relationship to the Platonic scale of nature about which so much was written in the sixteenth, seventeenth, and eighteenth centuries is quite evident. Shakespeare's monster Caliban is himself a literary forerunner of some of the incipient missing links which were to distort the scientific thinking of the nineteenth century—the century which, at the same time, was to enhance and modernize our conceptions of organic change and racial variation.

Caliban strikes the mind immediately as partly the artistically transmuted experience of the sixteenth century voyagers and partly an imagined link in that great scale of nature leading from inorganic matter up to man (2). Indeed, only some ten years after *The Origin of Species,* one of the Victorians, Daniel Wilson, in a now-forgotten book (3), devoted a lengthy essay to Caliban, referring to him as a "novel anthropoid of high type—such as on the hypothesis of evolution must have intermediately existed between the ape and man." He is "the half human link" superior, in the mind of Wilson, to the "degraded Bushman or Australian savage." With this latter expression we are introduced to another attempted paradigm of the nineteenth century—the

conception of other races as degenerate, as having their humanity measured by their remoteness from what Hugh Miller called the Adamic
center; namely, the Holy Land.

Having taken our cue from Shakespeare and the Victorians, we
may now ask what speculations from the past of the great voyagers
mingled with the preconceptions of Christian philosophy to partially
enchant the minds even of those scientists like Darwin and his circle,
who had perceived the progressive emergence of genuine novelty behind
the seeming stability of organic forms. Race and its mutability they
recognized, but their vision, paradoxically, was flawed by the distortions
inherited from the philosophical past which had made their feat of
insight possible.

Into this odd assemblage of conflicting ideas time will allow us
only a brief glimpse, but even that glimpse will reveal a very strange
reorientation of thought—the ladder of geological time drawn up, as it
were, from the vertical well of the past and lateralized within the world
of the present. This act, it should be emphasized, was carried out by
scholars protesting their intent of probing that same deep well of time.
Compared to the present abundance, however, their fossil resources were
pitifully meager. As a consequence, their entire scholarly tradition
impelled the Victorians into the enchanted realm where Caliban
beckoned. They were entranced by fantasies of living fossils and so-
called atavisms. In fact, these are with us yet in the shape of the
Himalayan snowmen. Frequently, when the Victorians thought they
saw the past, they were, in reality, looking upon a geographically differentiated present. They had forgotten Bacon's dictum that by art man
could become a god to man.

The stages in this long process of racial evaluation, which has so
beclouded the thinking of the last one hundred and fifty years, began
long before Darwin and can only be swiftly summarized here. It
begins with the carry-over into modern thinking of deep-rooted elements
of that ladder of existence or scale of nature which, to the devout Christian thinker, was an expression of God's infinite capacities and a mani-
festation of the unswerving continuity and stability of the universal
mind. This concept, whose history since the time of the Greeks has
been thoroughly explored by intellectual historians, contains in essence
an almost self-evident proposition: that there is in nature a scale of
organization running from the inanimate to animate bodies, and from

animate bodies, by increasing and continuous complexity, thence to man, and, less obviously, beyond him into the invisible realm of the spirit.

This ladder was conceived as static, having been frozen at the instant of creation. The unswerving conception of God's will was such that no link could change position with another link, and no single species could become extinct without endangering the entire creation. At first glance the scale and writings about it appear to have an evolutionary flavor, but the ladder is fixed within the short Christian time scale of a relatively brief cosmology. Nevertheless, aspects of this conception encouraged the naturalists' search for links in the ladder of life and thus promoted the growth of taxonomy and comparative anatomy. It has been remarked that the conception of the *scala naturae* nurtured the seeds of evolution and needed only augmented time and the idea of successive, animate emergence to be transformed into a genuine philosophy of evolution.

By the middle of the eighteenth century the static scale was, in Lovejoy's phrase, becoming temporalized. Voltaire speculated upon the unfilled gap between ape and man. D'Holbach wrote about the transitory nature of existing species: "Nature," he contended, "contains no constant forms." With the rise of deism in France, God's second book of revelation, that of nature, was being studied with increasing enthusiasm. This was not all, however. The early voyagers rounding the Cape of Good Hope to the Spice Islands of the Far East had run the gamut of the human scale. They had heard confused accounts of that strange forest ape man, the orang. Touching at the Cape, they had observed the impoverished cultures of Bushman and Hottentot. They had heard a glottal speech so distant from European tongues that its sounds were assumed to be monkey-like. The Hottentot had begun to fill a role he was long destined to play—that of a missing link between ape and man in the scale of nature.

Slowly, as the world-ranging voyagers brought home accounts of new peoples, the gap between man and ape would seem to narrow into a smooth transition for which the Western mind was well prepared. Strange races and barbaric cultures in inextricable confusion would seem to provide the ascending continuity that the ancient ladder of being demanded. Furthermore, that continuity made no demands upon the past. It represented, instead, an unbroken transition clearly observable within the existing order. These imaginary links merely filled out more satisfactorily for European man the unchanging universe in which he found himself.

Yet, as we have hinted, long before Darwin the thinkers of the eighteenth century had begun to suspect that emergent novelty lay somewhere at the heart of the static system their forerunners had perfected. The new instrument of comparative morphology would eventually be extended, like the genuine ladder that it was, into the depths of time. In Darwin's day, however, the world of the paleontologist was still a misty and uncertain realm. Time had been extended, and a natural mechanism of change postulated. Information on the human past was still hard to come by. The result, as I have previously intimated, was that almost the entire Darwinian circle, though they *talked* about man in the past, showed an amazing persistence in the extension of the old scale of nature into the present in order to deal with the new problems which beset them.

Wandering explorers would read into the faces of insular forest peoples the features of some ancestral anthropoid. Upon scant evidence the vocabularies of primitives would be judged meager, or their voices "a farrago of bestial sounds." Darwin, writing in the year of *The Origin of Species*, spoke of the "fine gradation in the intellectual powers of the Vertebrata, with one rather wide gap . . . between say a Hottentot and an Ourang, even if civilised as much mentally as the dog has been from the wolf" (4).

Somehow the vision of the age was distorted. In principle it had lengthened geological time and made way for the successive emergence of plant and animal novelty. When its scholars turned to man, however, they persisted in the old pattern of previous centuries. They encountered Caliban on a hundred leafy isles. On the lecturer's platform, in lieu of fossils, were ranked, as visible links in the human story, the chimpanzee, the Hottentot, and the Negro. Microcephalic idiots were regarded as genuine human atavisms. The artifacts and institutions of non-Western cultures were similarly ranked as living fossiliferous stages in the advance of Western society.

Darwin and his biological circle had an incalculable effect on the public of the Western world and upon its philosophical experience of the past. It is unfortunate that there were caught up in this mighty stream of thought many of the myths of race which were the product of an earlier and less enlightened era. These concepts have clung like burs in the minds of the lay public and have proved most difficult to eradicate even with the aid of the far more substantial information available to us today.

Where our prejudices are concerned, we find it easy to encapsulate ourselves in a past century. Nor, to be sure, is race the only human phenomenon upon which have been vented human spleen and aggression. In some ages men of common racial ties have spurned and murdered each other over religious differences more violently inflammatory than race. Worst of all, and perhaps indicative of some lurking mental shadow, man has not yet learned to evict from his uneasy psyche his sometimes fanatical zest for the promotion of a hidden myth of race where no consistent biological differences exist, where indeed a phantom, a mass hallucination has taken the place of white or black or yellow skin. Unnumbered millions of Caucasians died in the gas chambers of the Third Reich because of a deliberately fostered racial illusion. In the Orient, the Untouchables represent, in essence, a long-institutionalized body of people barely suffered to exist, who differ in no significant biological way from those around them.

Thus, in a brief survey of but one or two facets of the history of thinking about race, we may observe that, in the case of man, he may be biologically informed upon the subject, but this knowledge is not a certain check upon his emotions. As his numbers and his consequent irritations grow, there will always exist the danger that malicious infection from disturbed minds will cause the kind of momentary violence of alienation that I experienced on a Washington doorstep thirty years ago. I am sure that the memory of that incident persisted lifelong among my student friends. America today can ill afford such episodes. The tragedy that we face is the tragedy of all races. For whether we speak of black power, white power, or yellow power and mean by the term an encroachment on the rights of others, by just so much is the common humanity of all races diminished.

NOTES AND REFERENCES

1. Charles Darwin, *The Descent of Man* (2nd rev. ed., London, John Murray, 1888), I, 306.

2. In the middle of a humorous essay by Richard Cumberland (late eighteenth century) occur the following remarks, which suggest, even well before Darwin, the position of the great apes in the "scale" leading to man. "As I have also preserved a sketch of my famous Ourang-Outang, a thought has struck me, that with a few finishing touches he might easily be converted into a Caliban for the Tempest. . . ." *Observer*, No. 98, reprinted in Alexander Chalmers, ed., *The British Essayists, with Prefaces, Historical and Biographical* (2nd ed., London, J. Johnson, 1817), Vol. 39, p. 328.
3. Daniel Wilson, *Caliban: The Missing Link* (London, Macmillan and Co., 1873).
4. Francis Darwin, ed., *The Life and Letters of Charles Darwin* (London, John Murray, 1887), II, 211.

BENTLEY GLASS

The genetic basis of human races

In the course of a recent conversation Ernst Mayr and I agreed that probably no two of you sitting next to each other in the audience at this session would differ by fewer than several hundred genes. On the other hand, as Professor Dobzhansky has pointed out, the differences which distinguish human populations from one another, whether they are so distinct that we call them races or not, are expressed by the geneticist in terms of the frequencies of different genes; that is to say, some of you here are of blood group A, some are of blood group B, some are of blood group O. Knowing the nature of this population, I could predict rather well what percentage of each blood type would be present in a sample. Facing an audience in Tokyo instead of Washington, I would predict different frequencies of A and B and O. The difference is not that in Japan there are no individuals of type A or type O and only individuals of type B; quite the contrary, all three types are present in such a population, just as they are present here. The difference is that in Japan there would be more individuals in the audience of type B, and consequently fewer of types A and O. There are practically no populations in the world in which all three blood types of the A-B-O system are not represented, although among the Indians of North and South America before they became intermixed with other peoples, there seem to have been no individuals of type B.

Very few such all-or-none characteristics of a genetic nature distinguish the different major races of mankind. In contradistinction to the four hundred or so genes by which you differ from your neighbor, there are probably not more than a dozen different genes that it would be easy to specify as occurring in one race but not in others.

Races are subdivisions of a species. There is no real distinction between races, in the anthropological or zoological sense, and subspecies. Races (or subspecies) always are separated from each other in space or time. In other words, contemporaneous races or subspecies always are separated from each other geographically. Different races of the same species differ adaptively, as a rule. They may or may not show some degree of genetic isolation, that is, preferential breeding with mates of their own race, or of lessened fertility of the interracial mating or of the hybrids so produced. The analysis of race and population structure as factors in evolution owes much to R. A. Fisher (1), Sewall Wright (2), and J. B. S. Haldane (3).

The formation of races, through geographic isolation and adaptation by means of natural selection, up to a stage of marked morphological difference and complete barriers to direct gene exchange among them, is dramatically illustrated in Figure 1 by a chain of races described by R. C. Stebbins (4) in the California salamander, *Ensatina eschscholtzi*, in which the distributions of the end members of the chain overlapped with no apparent interbreeding. Only an interruption of the ring by extinction of one or more intermediate races is therefore required to complete the process of speciation.*

The ring or chain of races—"circular overlap" of geographic races in Mayr's terminology—enables us to arrive at a fairly satisfactory definition of a species on a biological or genetic basis. A sexually reproducing species undergoing geographic differentiation is isolated from other related species by the lack of interchange between the several gene pools of the species. On the other hand, races belonging to the same species, although somewhat differentiated by selection, can still experience gene flow between their populations, at least indirectly, through intermediate races.

* A brief note by Brown and Stebbins (5) indicates that there is some hybridization between the blotched and unblotched subspecies of *Ensatina* at the ends of the ring in Mill Canyon in southern California. That finding might seem to render the example inappropriate, but this is probably not so. Stebbins writes (personal communication) that further investigation by Brown, soon to be published, shows that hybrids are in fact rare between the extreme forms of the chain or ring. He states: "I feel at present that the Rassenkreis still can serve as a good example of circular overlap because of the apparent low frequency of genetic breakdown in southern California."

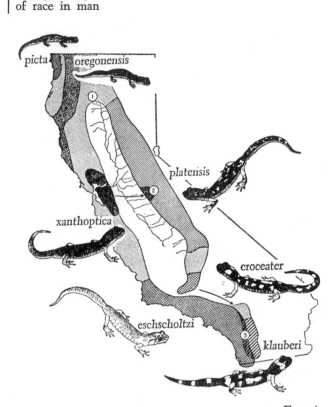

FIGURE I. SUBSPECIES OF THE SALAMANDER, *Ensatina
eschscholtzi*, IN CALIFORNIA. (COURTESY OF PROFESSOR
R. C. STEBBINS.)

The races of *Homo sapiens,* whether we lump them into a few
or split them into a great many, are clearly of geographic origin. There
is no evidence whatsoever of genetic isolation between them. Offspring
of interracial matings are unimpaired, if not superior, in vigor and
fertility. Consequently, we may conclude that within our present species, the process of speciation has not yet approached the stage at
which subspecies become full species.

The student of human genetics is therefore concerned mainly
with an analysis of early stages of speciation, with changes in allelic
frequencies brought about by mutation, selection, gene flow, or genetic
drift. The effects of each of these evolutionary factors are strongly
subject to modification by the sizes of the populations involved.

In the small populations of precivilized times, the effects of mutation would expectably be more diversifying than today. The probability that the same favorable mutation would arise in two small populations (breeding size, 250) within the same span of 25,000 years, or roughly 1000 human generations, is only 25 per cent if the gene has a mutation rate of 10^{-6} (one in a million). The probability that it becomes established in both populations is very much less. Consequently, in those early times favorable mutations would rarely, if ever, arise and become established in more than one population coincidentally. Today, on the contrary, our breeding populations are so large that any favorable mutation is quite likely to arise in every population quite frequently. In a population of breeding size 10^8 (100 million individuals; 200 million functioning gametes per generation), a mutation with a frequency of 10^{-6} will arise 200 times per generation.

Chance, in the form of random genetic drift, also has far more effect in small populations—in fact, it is significantly effective only in such populations. Abrupt and unpredictable shifts of allele frequencies occur in small populations and may cumulate over several generations in a "run of luck." Small populations therefore come to differ radically in their gene frequencies from the populations of their origin, and not only for the above reason but also because of the "founder effect." That is, whenever a new colony is established by a very few individuals, it cannot be fully and proportionately representative of the gene pool from which it is drawn. The large populations of today minimize these effects, except where culturally or religiously isolated groups of small size hold themselves strictly aloof from intermarriage with their neighbors (6).

Large populations are subject to a different kind of selection pressure than that operating on man's ancestors. In primitive times selection was probably largely for survival to adulthood. It involved such factors as lack of physical defects, good intelligence, and, especially, resistance to malnutrition and constitutional disease. With the crowding of man into villages and cities and the advent of agriculture, selection pressure must have lessened along these lines and increased along others, such as in resistance against infectious diseases. Today we have changed all that once again. Modern nutritional and medical standards have sharply lowered the death rate. Most babies in most countries now have at birth a life expectancy exceeding the reproductive period. Hence viability yields to fertility as the chief modern form of selection pressure. Crow (7) has shown that there are ample differences in fertility rates to serve as a new basis for selection.

Gene flow is probably the principal factor now reducing the differences between the gene pools of the various human races. Thus the gene pool of North American Negroes (socially defined) is now approximately 30 per cent derived from white ancestry (8, 9). In South America the amalgamation is considerably greater. The races are in fact disappearing, although the process will require thousands of years at present rates.

We should not deny that certain racial differences—physical, nutritive, immunological, and perhaps behavioral—are possibly adaptive, although this is difficult to prove in even a single case. Comparisons of relative superiority must be made on a common basis, but that very fact renders them invalid, since the superiority relates to adaptation to a particular set of conditions, to a particular environment, that is not the same for any two populations or races. We may be able to say that for a certain set of conditions one trait is superior (in viability or fertility) to another, but the superiority cannot be generalized. For a different set of conditions, if the traits are the "normal" differences of different races, superiority often will rest with the alternate one. The very complexity and changing nature of the environment assures that selection will itself foster a complex process of genetic adaptation.

Finally, it is clear that certain "normal" alleles, present in virtually all human races—as, for example, the A-B-O blood group alleles —are by no means exempt from selection, but interact most complexly (10). Thus it seems that in a population containing solely A and O blood types, the introduction of the typically Mongolian allele for B produces an improved balance of selective factors (11). It is not clear that the introduction of B into a population composed solely of type O would be equally advantageous. Pure B/O populations do not exist, although theoretically they might. Sickle-cell hemoglobin and thalassemia are detrimental enough to cause the death of homozygotes. However, in regions of endemic malaria—man's great killer in civilized times—both sickle-cell hemoglobin and thalassemia have become widely dispersed and have served to preserve populations threatened with extinction because normal hemoglobin is so tasty to the malaria plasmodium.

As the human races disappear, genetic differences will of course remain, but within a polyglot population, a composite gene pool. From the study of the phenomenon of race in man, so long as it exists, we can derive useful knowledge about the interplay of evolutionary factors and perhaps even foresee what genetic adaptations will be required in our changing world.

REFERENCES

1. R. A. Fisher, *The Genetical Theory of Natural Selection* (Oxford, Clarendon Press, 1930).

2. Sewall Wright, "Evolution in Mendelian Populations," *Genetics,* 16 (1931), 97–159; "Population Structure as a Factor in Evolution," in *Moderne Biologie: Festschrift zum 60 Geburtstag von Hans Nachtsheim* (Berlin, F. W. Peters, 1950), 275–87; and "The Genetical Structure of Populations," *Annals of Eugenics,* 15 (1951), 323–54.

3. J. B. S. Haldane, *The Causes of Evolution* (London, Longmans, Green and Co., 1932).

4. Robert C. Stebbins, "Intraspecific Sympatry in the Lungless Salamander *Ensatina eschscholtzi,*" *Evolution,* 11 (1957), 265–70.

5. Charles W. Brown and Robert C. Stebbins, "Evidence for Hybridization between the Blotched and Unblotched Subspecies of the Salamander *Ensatina eschscholtzi,*" *Evolution,* 18 (1965), 706–07.

6. Bentley Glass, Milton S. Sacks, Elsa F. Jahn, and Charles Hess, "Genetic Drift in a Religious Isolate: An Analysis of the Causes of Variation in Blood Group and Other Gene Frequencies in a Small Population," *American Naturalist,* 86 (1952), 145–59.

7. James F. Crow, "Mechanisms and Trends in Human Evolution," in Hudson Hoagland and R. W. Burhoe, eds., *Evolution and Man's Progress* (New York, Columbia University Press, 1962), 6–21.

8. Bentley Glass and C. C. Li, "The Dynamics of Racial Intermixture: An Analysis Based on the American Negro," *American Journal of Human Genetics,* 5 (1953), 1–20.

9. Arthur G. Steinberg, Rachel Stauffer, and Samuel H. Boyer, "Evidence for a Gm^{ab} Allele in the Gm System of American Negroes," *Nature,* 188 (1960), 169–70.

10. Alice M. Brues, "Selection and Polymorphism in the A-B-O Blood Groups," *American Journal of Physical Anthropology,* 12, n.s. (1954), 559–97.

11. Bentley Glass, "On the Evidence of Random Genetic Drift in Human Populations," *American Journal of Physical Anthropology,* 14, n.s. (1956), 541–56.

PAUL T. BAKER

The biological race concept as a research tool

Throughout time man's languages and the concepts that they embody have passed through a constant process of change. In recent years the biological concept of race has gone through somewhat radical changes and some scientists have even argued strongly that it is a useless fiction. Perhaps the most extended debate of the question occurred in *Current Anthropology* from 1962 until 1964 (1, 2, 3), and in preparation for this paper the *Current Anthropology* series of articles, comments, and letters were reviewed. They were clearly of high scientific quality, yet it appears that most of the authors, either explicitly or implicitly, were debating the reality of something called race. Surely such a controversy is meaningless in modern science. "Races" have no more or less reality than "chairs" since both are human informational constructs which will linguistically and conceptually persist only as long as they serve the purposes of their users. Among human biologists the concept of race has two functions: first, as a pedagogic device for teaching human variation and, second, as a research tool for investigating biological variation. As has been pointed out several times, this concept is not (outside of history) an essential tool for teaching, since variability in individual traits can be taught without reference to a grouping approach (4). Therefore, we may assume that, at least among biologists, the concept of race will become no more than a scientific antiquity like the pre-Socratic four elements unless it has utility as a research tool.

94

Race is a concept common to many disciplines concerned with animal biology, but it has been primarily in relation to man that controversies over this topic have been the most vehement. This paper will, therefore, be concerned with the race concept primarily as it is used in the research directions that can be loosely identified as human biology. Human biology research has generally the same goals as the rest of the scientific endeavor—that is, understanding and prediction. Of course, at the present state of knowledge this ultimate goal is seldom projected and immediate aims are most often presented as simple description or the elucidation of particular relationships. For most human biologists the underlying theory is mechanistic and evolutionary in principle.

To achieve these goals and test the multiple hypotheses of evolutionary theory, the human biologists have used a variety of methods which until recent years continued to diverge according to the primary discipline affiliation. Thus, physical anthropologists described human biological variability across space and time, human geneticists searched for specific human genes by twin and familial studies, while human physiologists searched for species-wide regularities in physiological functions. All of these activities continue, but there has also developed a group of investigators in these and allied disciplines who are dissatisfied with the traditional directions of their disciplines. Many physical anthropologists now believe that their activity must not be limited to description but must also be concerned with how populations became diversified in their biological characteristics and what the consequence of this biological variation is to function and performance. The human geneticist is involved in similar directions, while many human physiologists are now questioning why individuals and groups of individuals do not respond in the same way to stresses such as heat, cold, altitude, and trauma.

In this short treatment, only three disciplines have been emphasized, but similar trends have developed in many others, including nutrition, demography, medicine, and psychology. Such a trend for a communality of direction is unusual in the development of constantly fractionating science. Of more concern to this discussion are the methods of these scientists since they are significantly involved with the concept of race, not as defined by any extant system but as a rough measure of genetic distance in human populations. This concern is justified by the great emphasis being placed upon the comparative approach in present-day human biology research.

Perhaps the best guide to the direction in which human biology research will move during the next ten years is provided by the proposals of the Human Adaptability Project of the International Biological Programme (5). This project, which was originally planned by human biologists from several countries, is now being carried out by scientists from more than forty nations, with many countries already committed to detailed research programs. A detailed analysis of this project is not necessary to make the point. It is sufficient to note that basically the project depends upon the comparative approach to produce its major contribution to knowledge. The individual studies that will be undertaken may contain a minimum of comparison since some will be only the measurement of growth in Polish children or a multidisciplinary study of Eskimos. However, the major point of the project is that by the standardization of techniques and the exchange of data, we can better understand the extent, sources, and consequences of human biological variation.

The use of the comparative technique is by no means new. It has been the fundamental method of anthropology since its inception and has had widespread application in other disciplines. It may even be considered the basis of experimental research since an experiment depends on holding constant as many variables as possible while measuring the consequence of varying one parameter. In the past, the comparative approach has often been misused or misinterpreted by investigators in human biology. Thus the low-fat diets of some non-U. S. populations were once interpreted as the cause for the low incidence of atherosclerosis among these groups as compared to U. S. populations (6). Such an interpretation failed totally to recognize that these groups were also different from U. S. populations in genetics, aspects of the physical and biotic environments, and aspects of the cultural environment. Quite clearly the comparative method can be a misleading approach if carelessly applied. It is clear to most researchers now using this method that before coming to any conclusion they must consider all of the parameters of variation; among the most important of these are the genetic differences in human populations.

In the extended controversy over the subject of race, the concept has been attacked as of no value because it does not aid in a study of how and why particular known genes are distributed. This position appears partially justified, but it fails to cover the bulk of planned comparative research. What of the atherosclerosis example cited previously? There is no conclusive evidence on whether the human heterozygous genetic system contains genes which produce population differences in lipid metabolism, although such a possibility has been suggested (7). Thus, of the many directions which will be followed in lipid metabolism research, it is quite probable that someone will wish to further extend the comparative approach in order to find out whether genetically different human populations have the same or different responses to the ingestion of fats. When such research is planned the question will arise, What populations? If properly executed, the studies will give consideration to all aspects of the environment as well as the genetic characteristics of the populations, but since no other guidelines exist, it would be logical to begin the comparison with populations which have a maximal genetic distance.

In view of the need for genetic-distance measurement as a research tool, the prime problem becomes the best estimating system available. Several mathematical efforts in this direction have used known human gene systems (8, 9). There have also been efforts based on morphological differences, with the assumption that these relate to gene systems (10, 11). Both of these directions are worthwhile; but, considering what a small percentage of human genes are known and that external morphology is only a minor aspect of the complex human phenotype, it seems reasonable to suggest that racial taxonomic systems that are commonly based on a composite system may be better indications of genetic distance. This hypothesis may be partially tested at least by reference to genetic evolutionary principles.

From the principles of selection, drift—including the founder's principle—and gene flow, two general principles emerge. First, the greater the mating isolation of two populations, the greater is the probable genetic distance. This is a deceptively simple statement since mating isolation in man is an enormously complex problem. Of the isolating factors which are known, we may consider two, geographical distance and terrain. Yet the degree to which these geographical features isolate depends on the culture form. Water is a barrier without boats and a highway with them. Time of isolation is also a critical factor, as are a multitude of cultural characteristics. Indeed, a major developing research interest in the nature of isolating factors for human populations and gene systems has indicated the complexity of this problem.

As a second principle, it seems a supported hypothesis that the greater the difference in environment (physical, biological, and cultural), the greater the genetic difference in populations. This principle is rather simply derived from the nature of selection compounded by the fact that differences in the environment are also likely to act as gene flow barriers. From these two guidelines we may, therefore, derive the theoretical generalization that the greater the separation of two populations in mating distance, time, and environment, the greater is the genetic distance.

Of equal interest is the empirical finding that a similar generalization might be made about the ontogenetic process. Perhaps without a quantitative analysis of the evidence some human biologists may disagree, but it appears that when the sum of evidence is reviewed, the more disparate the environments in which individuals of the same genetic composition develop, the more disparate is the final product in terms of structure, function, and behavior. If this generalization should prove valid, the previous one about genetic differences could be extended to the statement that the phenotypic difference between populations produced by both phylogenetic and ontogenetic processes will generally be dependent on the amount of separation in mating distance, time, and environment. This generalization has limited significance for the distribution of single genes or single morphological traits such as weight or skin color, and I hope that it will not be attacked on the basis of exceptions. A great deal of printed space has been wasted in arguing against statistical generalities such as Bergman's rule by the citation of exceptions (12, 13, 14). Instead, the function of such a generalization should be to serve as a guideline for a human biologist who wishes to use the comparative approach as a first method for examining the degree and source of variability in a human biological characteristic.

Given the preceding sources for genetic diversity in man, it is possible to investigate whether the current racial classification systems and theoretical guidelines for estimating genotypic and phenotypic distance coincide. If we examine the reconstructed populations of man in the pre-Columbian era, enough evidence is now available to support some calculated guesses about how the world populations related at that time to the three guidelines of breeding isolation, time separation, and environmental variation. What follows is intended to suggest what such a comparison might find and is, of course, not a detailed effort to trace the relationships.

Breeding isolation

By the sixteenth century some populations for several millennia had been agriculturalists. This revolution had many effects on human breeding patterns. Because it led to faster transportation by means of pack animals, carriages, and large boats, it greatly increased the distance over which men could breed. But at the same time, the neolithic revolution gave rise to classes, castes, and other previously unknown social structures that channeled and restricted mating patterns. Thus, for some parts of the world, gene flow rates had increased, and new nongeographical factors had become of major importance to breeding isolation. Nevertheless, a number of studies on recent peasant groups have shown a rather smooth leptokurtic relationship between the probability of a couple mating and the distance between their childhood domiciles (15). From this evidence I would suggest that as of the fifteenth century, the four corners of the earth were also the four corners of breeding isolation and had been for a long time. To be less metaphorical, southern Africa, northern Europe, Australia, Japan, and the New World were probably the extremes of breeding isolation or gene flow. In between these points there were exceptions to this pattern so that the few feet of distance which separated an upper- and a lower-caste member in parts of India were greater, in terms of mating accessibility, than the miles between Hawaii and Tahiti.

Time separation

The fact that geographical distance in the year 1500 was a rough measure of breeding isolation did not mean that genetic distance corresponded, since man had made several major migrations into new geographical areas in the previous 2000 to 20,000 years, carrying his genes with him. The neolithic revolution had also provided a tremendous technological and population advantage to its bearers, allowing them to expand (16). Thus, as a result of recent migrations the Tierra del Fuego natives, though vastly isolated in immediate gene flow from

the New England Indians, probably were not too distant from them
genetically because of a comparatively recent common ancestry. On
the other hand, the neolithic revolution had affected gene flow so that
the southeast Asians were genetically linked by recent ancestry to the
Koreans, and the Mediterranean peoples had spread their genes far
into the European northland.

Environmental contrast

Of the three guidelines, environmental contrast is undoubtedly
the most difficult to describe, let alone reconstruct. Since the concept
of environment includes all the significant physical, biotic, and cultural
parameters, a competent analysis is obviously impossible. However, certain major environmental differences can be suggested. Because of oce-
anic or desert barriers there appear to have been fairly unique floral
and faunal assemblages in four world areas: Australia and New Guinea,
Africa (south of the Sahara), Eurasia, and the New World. There were
also, according to culture historians, at least three or four semi-independ-
ent centers for the neolithic revolution. These were the Near East, the
New World, southeast Asia, and possibly North China (17, 18). For
most environmental variables such as climate the distribution is too
complex to touch on in this paper. It can be noted that these rough
environmental areas also correspond to the breeding isolation zones.

Thus, the guidelines in relation to human populations as of
1500 have been summarized briefly and loosely. It is perhaps not surprising to note that they suggest that the genotypic and phenotypic
distances between human populations probably agree quite well with
some of the modern or even some of the ancient racial taxonomic systems.

This remark does not, I hope, suggest that any classificatory
system is likely now or in the future to be the ultimate tool for comparative human biology research. Indeed, racial classification systems
are at best interim structures for dealing with genetic and phenotypic
distances and should be replaced by quantitative systems. Even better,
it may be hoped that the comparative method will be replaced by the
more accurate method of mechanism analysis. However, neither of these
hopes is likely to materialize in the near future, and race is likely to
remain a useful concept in the science of human biology for many

decades even though it will, undoubtedly, be a constantly changing informational construct.

REFERENCES

1. Frank B. Livingstone, "On the Non-existence of Human Races," *Current Anthropology,* 3 (1962), 279.
2. Marshall T. Newman, "Geographic and Microgeographic Races," *Current Anthropology,* 4 (1963), 189–92.
3. C. L. Brace, "On the Race Concept," *Current Anthropology,* 5 (1964), 313–14.
4. Ashley Montagu, ed., *The Concept of Race* (New York, The Free Press, 1964).
5. J. S. Weiner, *International Biological Programme Guide to the Human Adaptability Proposals* (London, ICSU-SCIBP, 1965).
6. National Research Council, Food and Nutrition Board, *Dietary Fat and Human Health* (Washington, National Academy of Sciences, 1966).
7. J. Mayer, "Metabolism of the Adipose Tissue in the Hereditary Obese-Hyperglycemic Syndrome," in Kare Rodahl and Bela Issekutz, eds., *Fat as a Tissue* (New York, McGraw-Hill Book Co., 1964).
8. W. W. Howells, "Population Distances: Biological, Linguistic, Geographical and Environmental," *Current Anthropology,* 7 (1966), 531.
9. Walter M. Fitch and Emanuel Margoliash, "Construction of Phylogenetic Trees," *Science,* 155 (1967), 279–84.
10. C. R. Rao, *Advanced Statistical Methods in Biometric Research* (New York, John Wiley and Sons, 1952).
11. Jean Hiernaux, "La Mesure de la Différence Morphologique entre Populations pour un Ensemble de Variables," *L'Anthropologie,* 68 (1964), 559–67.
12. P. F. Scholander, "Evolution of Climatic Adaptation in Homeotherms," *Evolution,* 9 (1955), 15–26.
13. Ernst Mayr, "Geographical Character Gradients and Climatic Adaptation," *Evolution,* 10 (1956), 105–8.
14. P. F. Scholander, "Climatic Rules," *Evolution,* 10 (1956), 339–40.
15. L. L. Cavalli-Sforza, "Some Data on the Genetic Structure of Human Populations," *Proceedings of the Tenth International Congress of Genetics* (Toronto, University of Toronto Press, 1959), I, 389–407.

16. Frederick S. Hulse, "Some Factors Influencing the Relative Proportions of Human Racial Stocks," *Cold Spring Harbor Symposia on Quantitative Biology*, 22 (1957), 33–45.
17. Ralph Linton, *The Tree of Culture* (New York, Alfred Knopf, 1955).
18. Grahame Clark, *World Prehistory: An Outline* (London, Cambridge University Press, 1961).

ERNST MAYR

Discussion

What has struck me at this meeting up to now is the essential similarity of views, and also the fact that the various speakers have already emphasized the important points. If I can do anything it is to reemphasize some of the points that again and again are misunderstood.

The first question is: Are there races? Quite rightly all the speakers said that if you define races properly then, yes, there are races. Let me, as a zoologist, say that when you look at animals (and a botanist finds the same thing with plants), there is hardly a species that does not also have geographic races. If you look at the genetic structure of populations, this is of course exactly as it ought to be. Every locality is different from every other locality; every individual, whether human individual or individual of plants or individual of animals—I'm speaking now of sexually reproducing species—every individual is genetically different. Therefore, with different localities having different environments and different selective factors, every population will be different. And the only question is, to what extent is it useful to group together such local populations and call them races? It is at this point that we have to become critical.

The important thing is to realize that race *is* a populational phenomenon; it *is* a statistical phenomenon; it is *not* a typological phenomenon. If we look at extremely different populations, we have no problem at all saying that they are different races. But if we look at some recent textbooks on physical anthropology, we find that in one textbook they recognize five human races, in the next textbook they recognize sixty-five human races. Races there are; how to delimit them, how to draw the line between them is not only difficult, it is impossible.

103

I am reminded of an apocryphal story about the American newspaperman who went to Haiti and had an interview with the President. They started to talk about Haiti and its population, and most indiscreetly the American newspaperman asked the President what percentage of the people were white. And the President of Haiti said, "Oh, about 95 per cent." The American newspaperman looked a little puzzled and said, "Well, how do you define white?" And the President of Haiti said, "How do you define colored?" And the American newspaperman said, "Well, of course, anybody with Negro blood is colored." Said the President: "Well, that's exactly our definition, too: anybody with white blood is white."

I tell this just to point out the difficulties of typological definitions. At the same time I agree with Professor Dobzhansky and virtually all the other speakers: there are mean differences and very often, particularly when we have well-segregated groups, it is possible to describe these differences in statistical terms. These differences then have a very definite meaning provided we are at all times aware of the fact that they are statistical and not typological differences.

For the last twenty years I have been flogging that horse of the differences between typological interpretations and populational ones, and every once in a while my friends tell me that I am flogging a dead horse. But then I read something by somebody else, and I realize that maybe it's a good idea to continue flogging this horse. For instance, I am just a little scared of this idea of defining races in terms of genetic distance because genetic distance immediately becomes one particular figure, one particular term; and then somebody immediately might want to use this in a typological sense, as has been done in recent racist literature.

To illustrate my point, let me give you a strictly imaginary example: Take a sample of 1000 young American Negro males and 1000 young American white males, let them run the hundred-yard dash and then take the mean time of the two samples. For the sake of argument (I haven't the faintest idea how fast a hundred-yard dash is run), suppose that the average for the Negro males turned out to be 13.4 seconds and for the white Americans, 13.5 seconds. A typologist would say, "You see, the Negroes run faster than the whites." We all know the absurdity of this because the overlap between the two samples would probably be well over 90 per cent. This is important to stress at all times: if we ever mention mean differences between population groups which are labeled as races, let us realize that there is this tremendous overlap, and that to compare them in terms of mean values is not merely misleading but actually quite pernicious.

So much for the necessity for the populational approach. Now let me just say one or two additional things. Several speakers in Session I mentioned the possibilities of selection in even a rather small gene pool and how, without major changes in this gene pool, tremendous phenotypic effects could be achieved in comparatively few generations. It has always seemed to me that we haven't stressed enough what natural selection or evolution has done in the comparatively short time since the hominid line branched off from the line that leads to the African apes, to the chimpanzee-gorilla group. Serum proteins, hemoglobin, chromosomes, and any number of other chemical constituents of the body are still virtually identical in man and the African apes. Even in the blood groups, the differences are not very dramatic. Here we have some relatives of man that are definitely different species, even a different genus, and yet are still close to man, to the hominoid line, in a great deal of their genetic composition. The tremendous deviation, the humanization of the hominid line, was thus achieved by evolution and natural selection with only part of the genetic constitution, part of the genotype. We have to remember this sort of thing whenever we talk in terms of natural selection. Different evolutionary rates for different attributes are even more characteristic for races than for species.

Now let me say one final thing: We who believe in populations and stress the importance of not thinking in terms of mean differences and not exaggerating mean differences should not fall into the equally erroneous extreme of thinking of the total identity of everybody. As Professor Dobzhansky has so rightly pointed out, it is the very fact of the absence of identity among human individuals and the overlap and partial nonidentity of human groups that makes the principle of equality so important. If all of us were identical there would be no sense whatsoever in an ethical principle of equality. As the late J. B. S. Haldane stressed so many times, we can never have true equality if we do not have equality of opportunity. And we cannot have equality of opportunity, considering the fact that we do not have genetic identity among people, if we do not provide a diversified environment, that is, if we do not provide multiple opportunities to take care of the different aptitudes of different people.

ETHEL TOBACH

Discussion

We have now heard two of the three sessions of this symposium. Two issues strike me as relevant almost immediately: first, what is the relationship between the two sessions, indeed the three sessions? Does the discussion about genetic and behavioral analyses contribute to our thinking about the concept of race as a biological phenomenon and about the concept of race as a social phenomenon?

From this set of questions I am led to the second issue, raised by Drs. Hirsch, Mayr, and Dobzhansky: the importance of differentiating between typological conceptualization and the population approach. Dr. Hirsch contributed importantly by designating the heredity-environment dichotomy as a pseudo question. It seems to me that the contrast of the typological and population approaches presents the same type of dichotomy. Dr. Birch's discussion proposed a theoretical orientation that deals with both issues. I spoke of the theory in this morning's session, but I believe it warrants repetition: the concept of levels of integration.

As Birch and T. C. Schneirla have applied the theory to behavioral phenomena, it emphasizes the fusion and continuous interdependent action of mechanisms and processes on many levels of organization, and integrates different levels of organization by intensifying and extending the concept of experience. In Schneirla's terms, experience is effective stimulation on all levels, including the biochemical coding in the genoma.

Dr. Eiseley's historical review of the philosophical and theological antecedents of the concept of levels of integration might lead one to consider the concept as rather static and perhaps not helpful in resolving the dilemma which has been posed for us. Recently, however, a most critical modification has come about by the introduction of Schneirla's concept of development, or historicity. The intercourse of these two concepts—levels of organization and development—has made the concept of levels of integration dynamic.

Dr. Eiseley's presentation of some of the history of the concept of race provides a useful background for the biological construct so thoughtfully discussed by Dr. Glass. Most pertinent to the problem before us was Dr. Glass's analysis of the shift in the form of selection pressures from resistance to stress to fertility. This was brought about by man's neural plasticity and ability to change and control his environment. Other examples of such change on the biological level may indicate some possibility for changing the human social level by that same plasticity and ability.

To implement this change, serious attention must be paid to Dr. Baker's statement that on the human informational level, the concept of race will persist as long as it has validity. A concept which is valid in one area, in this instance on the biological level, is not necessarily valid on another. On the human social level, I believe, the construct of race is not defensible by any of the acceptable criteria of validity testing. What is the comparative method that Dr. Baker spoke about? The comparative method deals not only with the description of the differences and similarities of variables and parameters but also requires the understanding of the processes on all levels of organization which may be relevant to these similarities and differences. As Dr. Birch pointed out earlier today, behavioral patterns may look alike but may be derived from distinguishably different processes. I do not share Dr. Baker's view of the future of scientific thinking and language. I think we can affect the social impact of our scientific knowledge by asking valid questions that can be experimentally answered. One approach that will yield such valid questions emphasizes the study of the development of behavior on different levels of organization and integration. As Dr. Gordon proposed this morning, there is a special need in today's evolving society to conduct investigations of the development of behavior and of how such knowledge can be used to modify human socially maladaptive processes, rather than to conduct demonstrational, descriptive types of investigations, stressing differences or similarities among individuals.

The point that Drs. Mayr and Dobzhansky make about identity

and equality exemplifies the usefulness of the levels concept. The distinction between identity and equality is most understandable and clear within the context of the doctrine of levels of integration. The concept of race on the *biological* level is understandable and logically defensible on every ground (nonidentical does not mean superior or inferior). But what is the relevance of this operational concept on the biological level to the ill-defined concept of race on the social human level, where racial nonidentity most frequently carries with it connotations of superiority and inferiority?

Each level has its own laws, techniques, and requirements for fact-finding and interpretation of those facts. The biologist's field and laboratory methods for studying infrahuman organisms cannot be applied without modification to the study of human phenomena. Human social behavior subsumes all preceding biological levels of organization and processes. For the human species, the concept of race may be relevant at the *physiological* level, as for example, differences in blood type. The validity of the construct of race on the human *behavioral* level is put into further doubt by the experience of those who study animals other than man. The science of animal behavior has not yet been able to clarify the relationship between the biochemical processes of genetics on the molecular level, the developmental processes on the physiological level, and the behavioral processes on the level of social organization. It becomes questionable then from the point of view of the concept of levels of integration whether the construct of race can have value for understanding human behavior.

If our ignorance is profound on the infrahuman level, can it be less on the human level?

PAUL T. BAKER

Supplementary remarks

I would like to clarify my remarks on genetic distance in answer to Dr. Mayr's comments. I was not suggesting that we should have race classification based on genetic distance. I was saying that genetic distance is a useful tool, and insofar as a racial classification system conformed to genetic distance, it would be useful. I think that his example of runners demonstrates the point I was suggesting; if we found such a difference between two populations, we should then undertake a long series of research studies to identify the source of the difference. Hopefully, we would get down to a study of the mechanism rather than this very amorphous thing of genetic distance.

I would also like to clarify what I said would cause retention of the word race or the concept of race. Validity is a word that has very little meaning to me because it is a human-defined concept, just as race is a human-defined concept. Hence, the only thing I am saying is that as long as the race concept is useful to science in some way, it will persist in scientific literature. The minute the concept is not useful as a research tool, it will disappear.

One final comment on the animal behaviorists: I find their work very fascinating, and to me the major contribution of the ethological approach to anthropology has been to dispel an old myth, namely, that if we could raise children in isolation from all stimuli and then test their behavior, we would find out what was truly genetic and what was not. The chick example that was given in Session I is a beautiful illustration of the fact that although a piece of information is transmitted genetically, it may still require an appropriate environment to manifest itself.

BENTLEY GLASS

Supplementary remarks

I would like to take the opportunity to emphasize one point that is often a subject of considerable misunderstanding. In general, people tend to suppose that racial differences of a genetic nature relate in a simple and direct way to their adaptiveness or adaptive character. In fact, because of the many biochemical steps which occur between the initial action of a gene and the final visible result of its product, the differences in the final product may not be the real source of the adaptive differences between the genetic characteristics. The visible effects may be mere by-products—a simple deposition of waste material, for example—that are not related at all to the ability of the individual to survive and reproduce with a certain level of fertility in the usual environment.

We know from genetic studies with many different species that you can find significant differences in viability and fertility between two genetic strains that are not related to the visible effects of those genes. So, if it seems that red hair in the Australian aborigines has some superior virtue because, following its relatively recent origin, it has spread and become a general characteristic of these tribes, that doesn't actually mean that it is the red hair itself that is a particular adaptive characteristic. The adaptive feature may be some other effect of the gene that incidentally results in the change of hair color. Gene changes, gene differences, as a rule have multiple effects. We must beware of attaching significant adaptive character to any one of these without positive evidence.

110

THREE ✹ SOCIAL AND PSYCHOLOGICAL ASPECTS OF RACE

DWIGHT J. INGLE

The need to investigate average biological differences among racial groups

I am among those who prefer, when possible, to attend to individuality rather than racial origin. The ideal is to judge each person according to abilities, drives, behavior, and the assumption of duties rather than as a member of a group. The need to study average biological differences among groups arises when social action is based on group identification. So-called racial groups are of mixed origins, and no physical or behavioral trait is found exclusively in one race. The range of individual differences within a racial group is far greater than average group differences. However, the genes representing traits that are important in human affairs are not randomly and equally distributed among racial groups. The hopes of man must be compatible with his biological nature as well as his culture, for these are different aspects of the whole man.

A race has certain genes and gene combinations that are more frequent in it than elsewhere, but not confined to it. Some advocates of the view that average biological differences among races are not important to social action move from the fact that race is not clearly defined to an effort to prune the word from our vocabulary, so that we cannot talk about or investigate these problems, and hence to the conclusion that the problems do not exist. By the same perversion of logic,

113

it could be claimed that cancer, equally difficult to define, does not exist
and should not be studied.

Those who oppose the investigation of biological differences
among races do not hesitate to study environmental differences and to
recommend social action on the basis of racial identity rather than individuality. Of course the sensitive question is whether or not there is
any biological basis for the disadvantage Negroes experience as a racial
group in America and throughout the world. In discussing this question, I do not suggest that efforts to improve environment, to correct
cultural handicaps, and to ensure equal rights and opportunities be
withheld until there is better information on the biology of race.

There are important average differences in the school and job
achievements of whites and Negroes, and since social actions are taken
on the basis of the dogma that these differences are caused solely by
differences in environment, it becomes important to inquire into the
validity of this belief. I am opposed to racism, including reverse racism.
I am opposed to those social pressures by racists, both varieties, which
force the Negro to identify himself with his race rather than with his
social class or as an individual.

The question of average racial differences in genetic endowment
is important for the following reasons. First, both types of racists seek
to place individuals in schools, jobs, and housing on the basis of racial
identity rather than of abilities, interests, drives, and behavioral standards. Second, some social reformers urge the interbreeding of races as
a means of solving racial conflict. This biological proposal should not
be encouraged until it is known with certainty that it carries no risk
to the future of man. Are there any biological bases for the failure of
nations governed by Negroes and mulattoes to become self-sufficient
and creative? Third, if it is important that Negroes as a group should
gain equality of achievement as well as equal rights and opportunities
—I believe that this is a just goal—one necessary means to achieve
true equality may well be biological, that is, by positive eugenics or by
biological engineering when effective means are developed.

Studies on laboratory animals and on man (1, 2, 3) have shown
beyond reasonable doubt that ability to learn and reason has a genetic
basis and that environment is also important. There is no agreement
as to the relative importance of heredity and environment, for their
interactions evolve into Gestalten having no unambiguously distinguish-

able origins; the evidence on the relative importance of genetic endowment and the complex pattern of environmental causes is indirect.

There are large numbers of studies (4), many faulty in some respects, showing that Negroes on the average perform significantly less well than whites on objective tests of intelligence and school achievement. When delinquents, criminals, and homeless whites and Negroes are compared, the average differences are substantial and significant. Negro children who have had no experience with slums, poverty, or segregated schools do less well, on the average, than do white children. When Negro pupils are compared with whites of the same socioeconomic class, the average differences in test performance are commonly still substantial (4). It may be that the groups were only superficially equated. There are a few studies in which no significant difference was found. Much has been made of these atypical findings to support the claim that when environments are similar, test performance and achievement of whites and Negroes become similar. There is a glaring error of logic in such reasoning. Performances on tests and cultural and socioeconomic standing are interrelated because cultural and socioeconomic advancement depends in part upon intelligence. Therefore, a sample that is atypical with respect to one variable will be atypical with respect to the other two. It has been argued that because the Negro is handicapped by job discrimination, he must have higher intelligence than the white in order to reach the same socioeconomic level.

Comparisons (5) of the test performance of white and Negro recruits in World War I revealed that Negro recruits from certain northern states did better on the average than white recruits from certain southern states. The use of such comparisons, without emphasis on the better performance of northern whites and the poorer performance of southern Negroes, is an example of failure to embrace the concept of the controlled study. Protagonists of the view that these data proved that average racial differences in test performance were caused by environment neglected two additional relevant facts. First, the data represented men actually recruited into the army; the percentage of Negroes found unqualified for recruitment and thereby excluded was far higher than that of whites. Second, in southern states a higher percentage of white than Negro men had become officers, and their test scores were not included with those of the noncommissioned recruits. Relevant to these considerations are the figures released by the U. S.

Office of Education on the rate of failure on the psychological tests
for induction into the armed forces; 67.5 per cent of all Negroes failed
the test, as compared to 18.8 per cent of all non-Negroes, between June
1964 and December 1965. The data were reported as a measure of
environmental inequality,* and the possibility of a biological basis for
differences in test performance was not suggested.

A few studies (6) of simple motor learning in infants and young
children have shown that the Negro child performs as well as or better
than the white child. Such tests do not measure intelligence. There
is a general tendency for the difference in achievement between white
and Negro children to increase as they grow older. One view is that
the average decline of IQ of Negroes results from substandard schooling and increased experience with social discrimination. An alternative
hypothesis is that this decline is due in part to a genetically based difference in maturation of ability to learn and manipulate abstract ideas.

In a widely quoted study (7) involving a culture-fair test of
mental ability, a graduate student at the University of Chicago found
that white-Negro differences in test performance were much smaller
than is commonly found with standard intelligence tests. But the culture-fair test had not been validated by any of the means found useful
in test construction. There was no satisfactory evidence for internal
consistency of the test, and the method used to sample the children
of the city schools was inadequate. There have been other such studies
with similar faults.

One requirement for proof of a proposition is that the hypothesis
lead to control of the process under study. If the differences in test
performance and school achievement of whites and Negroes could be
abolished by control of the environment, the argument would be all
but won. Pilot experiments are possible. Current programs of preschool
training and school enrichment are not perfect models of what could
be tried, but it is frequently claimed that Negro-white differences in
test performance can be abolished by such programs. The results of
recent and current studies are frequently reported only in the lay press,
and it is impossible to obtain a detailed account of all the relevant
conditions with a complete summary of data. Not all groups involved
in such studies show improved test performance. Unless the results are
favorable, they are unlikely to be reported. The children are sometimes

* An excellent illustration of the *post hoc, ergo propter hoc* fallacy.

volunteers or are those judged most likely to profit by special training. There may be further selection when dropouts and absentees are excluded at the time of retesting. The identity of the pupil is not always recorded although needed for test-retest comparisons. The problem of experimenter bias, including the use of "fudge factors," is sometimes uncontrolled. When improvement is noted, is it due to extra motivation, coaching, practice, or accrued test wisdom? What is the meaning of improved test performance? Does the improvement endure? Is the child now improved in respect to other achievements based on ability to reason? It is rare to find a study that has compared both Negro and white children before, during, and after identical preschool programs and early enrichment and training.

Significant differences in test performance and school achievement between whites and Negroes persist among children having experience only with integrated schools (8). These differences are found in the schools of villages, towns, and small cities of the North where there are no slums, little unemployment, and no segregation in schools. The results of Project Talent (8), an extensive study of pupil and school characteristics in relation to the percentage of Negroes in school enrollment, show a strong tendency for average scores on aptitude and achievement tests to decrease as the percentage of Negroes increases. This is true of southeastern, eastern, and northern areas. Little difference in test scores was found among schools serving children from low-, medium-, and high-quality housing.

The results of a series of studies initiated by the U. S. Office of Education and published under the title *Equality of Educational Opportunity* (9) showed that in tests of school achievement and of verbal and nonverbal abilities approximately 85 per cent of Negro scores were below the white average and that the highest regional average score for Negroes was below the lowest for whites. The studies, imperfect in important respects, revealed little evidence that equality of educational opportunity can increase the equality of educational achievement.

It is claimed that a variety of psychological factors resulting from social discrimination and segregation may cause feelings of fear, inferiority, hopelessness, and hostility which are detrimental to the test performance and achievement of Negroes. Has the Negro been handicapped to a greater extent by these factors than have Asians and Jews in America? If so, how? What became of the "golden complex" of the 1920s, the Adlerian view that inferiority feelings are basic to creativity? Ideas are in and out of fashion. Will those currently in vogue withstand rigorous tests of claims to knowledge? In the history of immigration each newly arrived minority group has been misjudged as to racial qualities and abilities. It can be postulated that Negroes are similarly misjudged, but to claim that this hypothesis is proved by history is to commit the error of inferring universal statements from singular ones. The history of the Negro in America is not strictly analogous to that of any other immigrant group.

It is frequently claimed that intelligence tests are useless, especially by those who do not wish to accept conclusions supported by test results. Yet test scores correlate well with other measures of ability to reason abstractly and are useful in predicting school and job success. The predictive value of objective tests is just as high for Negroes as for whites. If these tests are without value, then upon what bases has it been proved that whites and Negroes are, on the average, equally endowed biologically?

So specious is the argument and so faulty the evidence given in support of this conclusion, and so consistently do Negroes, on the average, score significantly below whites on objective tests and in school achievement, that it seems plausible, even probable, that the dogma is incorrect. But all the evidence is indirect; the genes affecting intelligence have not been mapped or otherwise identified. Some genetic defects leading to metabolic errors that affect intelligence are known but are probably not bases for individual differences in intelligence among healthy individuals. There is evidence that early experiences have enduring effects upon biology and behavior; it is claimed that in laboratory animals learning experiences can affect the growth of the brain. There are many hypotheses whereby average white-Negro differences in test performance and school achievement could be explained without assuming a genetic basis for the difference.

I believe that better studies, even critical studies, are possible. Why have some groups of social scientists issued manifestoes asserting that the issue is closed? Why do some social scientists claim that their discipline alone has the right to deal with these questions and to withhold relevant information from members of other disciplines and from the public? Why is further research and debate discouraged and even calumniously attacked? Why are school children, college students, political leaders, and the public taught that all races are equal in respect to the biological bases of intelligence? The 1964 UNESCO proposals on the "Biological Aspects of Race" (10) said:

> The peoples of the world today appear to possess equal biological potentialities for attaining any civilizational level. Differences in the achievements of different peoples must be attributed solely to their cultural history.

The report of a study on *The Negro Family* (11) by the Federal Office of Policy Planning and Research provides a typical statement:

> There is absolutely no question of any genetic differential. Intelligence potential is distributed among Negro infants in the same proportion and pattern as among Icelanders or Chinese or any other group.

The subordination of science to social and political theory was never more vigorously pursued in the Soviet Union even during the heyday of Lysenkoism. I do not imply that the attempt to substitute closed systems of belief for the free pursuit of knowledge is the invention of the Communists. It is as old as history and was embraced by a well-known extremist of recent times.

> Science is a social phenomenon, and like every other social phenomenon is limited by the injury or benefit it confers on the community. . . . The idea of free and unfettered science . . . is absurd.

Who said this? Adolf Hitler! (12)

The 1967 report on race and the public schools issued by the U. S. Commission on Civil Rights recommends far more extensive pressures by government to force the integration of schools. A possible genetic basis for the school problems of some Negro pupils and the need to attend to individuality are not mentioned in the report. If the assumption as to the all-important role of environment in determining human nature and school progress is incorrect, the attempt will go awry. Wise efforts to guide integration on the basis of individuality have been a successful means in achieving equality of rights and opportunities for many Negroes. But when desegregation is brought about by blind social pressures or the forced random mixing of racial groups, schools and neighborhoods are commonly downgraded and *resegregation* occurs. It is my opinion that some, not all, interventions by social engineers are fostering, not curing, social malignancy.

These are moral issues involving the rights of individuals to private judgments, freedom of association, the right to be safe in person, and the right to the pursuit of happiness. Some persons fear that racists would misuse knowledge of average racial differences. I have seen no evidence that racists, either variety, are interested in truth. Knowledge can be misused, but ignorance cannot cure. We seek knowledge, not in order to discriminate against the disadvantaged, but in order to aid intelligently their advancement.

REFERENCES

1. H. H. Newman, F. N. Freeman, and K. J. Holzinger, *Twins: A Study of Heredity and Environment* (Chicago, University of Chicago Press, 1937). See also James Shields, *Monozygotic Twins* (New York, Oxford University Press, 1962).
2. L. Erlenmeyer-Kimling and Lissy F. Jarvik, "Genetics and Intelligence: A Review," *Science*, 142 (1963), 1477–79.
3. Steven G. Vandenberg, "Contributions of Twin Research to Psychology," *Psychological Bulletin*, 66 (1966), 327–52.
4. For review see: Anne Anastasi, *Differential Psychology* (3rd ed., New York, The Macmillan Co., 1958), and Audrey M. Shuey, *The Testing of Negro Intelligence* (2nd ed., New York, Social Science Press, 1966).
5. Otto Klineberg, *Characteristics of the American Negro* (New York, Harper and Brothers, 1944).
6. A. R. Gilliland, "Socio-Economic Status and Race as Factors in Infant Intelligence Test Scores," *Child Development*, 22 (1951), 271–73.
7. Robert D. Hess, "Controlling Culture Influence in Mental Testing: An Experimental Test," *Journal of Educational Research*, 49 (1955), 53–58.
8. G. R. Burket, *Selected Pupil and School Characteristics in Relation to Percentage of Negroes in School Enrollment* (Washington, Project Talent Office, 1963).

9. James S. Coleman et al., *Equality of Educational Opportunity* (Washington, Government Printing Office, 1966).

10. "Biological Aspects of Race," *UNESCO Courier* (April, 1965), 8–11.

11. Office of Policy Planning and Research, *The Negro Family* (Washington, U. S. Department of Labor, 1965), 35.

12. Hermann Rauschning, *Hitler Speaks: A Series of Political Conversations with Adolf Hitler on His Real Aims* (London, T. Butterworth, 1939), 220.

MORTON H. FRIED

The need to end the pseudoscientific investigation of race

Despite the sharp decline of interest in studies of human raciation among scientists best qualified to pursue such research, laymen and amateurs, often joined by scientists from nonanthropological or non-biological disciplines, continue to apply inappropriate methods to a variety of incorrectly formulated problems. The object of the studies that I have in mind can be phrased most charitably as the discovery of the presence, nature, and degree of differences in intelligence, ability, or achievement endowment between very large aggregates of people that are usually termed races. Most, although not all, of those who pursue such investigations declare themselves friends of all parties concerned. Quite often, the purpose of the study is declared to be amelioration of the human condition, including, marvelous to say, reduction of tensions and hostilities in the present racial crisis. But the unpleasant point of this paper is that the use of racial constructs in such studies is destructive and antisocial; it is also currently antiscientific. I believe that continued unfounded use of racial constructs will lead to further deterioration in social relations at various levels, ranging from personal to international, although I am in no position to predict that the contrary practice will by itself induce any general improvements.

In addition to the motives for racial educability studies already mentioned, there is another set, much more difficult to deal with, which might go under the general heading of the "autonomy of science." By this I mean to imply that the ultimate impulse for the study is asserted to be knowledge for its own sake, the desire to discover something not yet known. Proponents of this view believe that no limitations should be placed upon science, and the corollaries would seem to be (a) that no studies of scientifically valid design should be inhibited; and (b) that no scientist acting within reasonable competence should be restrained in his pursuits by what is usually called "social responsibility." Let us turn first to the studies that I have characterized as pseudoscientific.

The world has rarely been treated to panoramas of human violence and destruction except for the loftiest motives, such as the good of mankind. In similar vein, contemporary racists, wherever they arise, claim that their intended separation of races is for the general benefit. As a matter of fact, they claim universal benefits to flow from their schemes, benefits for all, including those who will bear stigma and suffer discrimination and exclusion.

Our contemporary phenomenon of racism is historically intertwined with institutionalized slavery, which is now almost but not quite extinct. It is instructive, therefore, to note that in the nineteenth-century endeavor to eliminate slavery strong use was made of theology, then still dominant in the realm of ideology. There was also a strong proslavery position couched in theological terms and specifically based on biblical interpretations. Although such arguments still survive, they linger almost entirely in educationally impoverished and anti-intellectual sectors of society. The theological arguments sustaining slavery have long since been replaced in educated and intellectual circles by arguments that have the superficial appearance of scientific pronouncements. That is, they are based on a variety of studies which, especially to the layman, seem impeccably scientific. The characteristic form of such a study is an inquiry into comparative scores achieved on a variety of psychological tests administered to sample populations of different racial backgrounds. Although studies of this kind have come a long way from the crudities of thirty or forty years ago, the growth of certain kinds of sophistication has not diminished the four basic faults which render them pseudoscientific at best:

1. Little progress has been made with the tests themselves, except those that frankly measure achievement rather than intelligence or ability potential.

2. While older tests were scored and interpreted without regard to cultural differences among respondents, modern tests usually are acknowledged to be culture-bound. The shift of emphasis from intelligence to achievement sometimes is allowed to obscure the significance of cultural variation in background, as when the lack of achievement motivation is offered as a racial characteristic in and of itself.

3. The so-called racial background of individual respondents and respondent populations is invariably derived in ways that show no resemblance to the means used by specialists in genetics. In other words, the actual genetic background of the subjects is usually uncontrolled in a truly technical sense.

4. Absolutely no study yet done on a so-called racial sample of human population adequately links intelligence, potential ability, educability, or even achievement to a specifiable set of genetic coordinates associated with any aggregate larger than a family line or perhaps lineage.

The matter which lies at one focus of our symposium, it seems to me, can be summed up by saying that pseudoscientific investigations of race can be recognized as such without difficulty because they cannot define the entities they wish to study with any reasonable degree of precision. Curiously, they must revert to conceptions of race found among laymen. Frequently racial sorting is done on the basis of the subjects' self-classification or the opinion of somebody in authority, perhaps a teacher or even the lay-investigator. Where information is given about criteria of assortment, one usually finds that skin color has been the sole or the dominant criterion. As a consequence, most available studies of racial differences in latent ability imply direct correlation between the genetics of skin color and the genetics of intelligence.

Let me be more specific about this problem of defining racial entities in studies which presume to relate race and some other variable. One of the standard works in the repertory of racists is *The Testing of Negro Intelligence* by Audrey M. Shuey (1). The definition of "Negro" or "colored" is the single most crucial item that Shuey must face; yet this is how she does it (2):

> We shall employ the terms *Negro* and *colored* interchangeably and may use the expression *race difference* when it applies to a

recognized difference between white and Negro Americans. Although many psychologists would agree with Herskovits . . . that the American Negro does not represent a pure racial group but rather a group with more-or-less African ancestry, yet they rather consistently refer to Negro-white differences as *racial differences*. The justification for this lies no doubt, as [Henry E.] Garrett indicates . . . , in the fact that except for small groups of transitional types, the American Negro constitutes a recognizable and clearly defined group, the criterion of membership in which group being that of more-or-less African ancestry.

Absolutely nothing is done by Shuey to demonstrate the recognizability or precise definition of the group. Also, consideration of the sample studies she collected for the 1958 publication indicates that very few of the 170 publications she consulted stated how their subjects were selected. Of the studies which describe how the racial identification was made, most relied upon simple divisions based on color, sometimes aided by color wheels or other devices but usually made by eye. Only the rarest study sought to obtain genealogical data, and the methods used in these very occasional studies verge on the ludicrous by standards of ethnography.

Indeed, most of these reports are unconsciously funny. A well-known study made in the 1920s by C. B. Davenport (3), for example, divided a sample of 200 Jamaicans into *Blacks* and *Browns* and then proceeded to determine "their physical characteristics," such as nasal breadth, hair form (measured by the diameter of the curl), interpupillary span, cephalic index, skin color (determined by the color top method), breadth of pelvis, and length of arm span. Comparable measurements were made on adult members of an isolated "white" community whose German ancestors had come to the island about four or five generations earlier and who had "carefully preserved their genealogical records." Note that the intricate morphological computations took place *after* the groups were differentiated and did not constitute any basis for differentiating them.

Actually, the most painstaking studies in terms of defining racial aggregates and specifying the criteria of selection have been virtually without exception the studies of anthropologists or psychologists critical of correlation of racial identification and intelligence or other socially valued variable. An example is the study by John E. Codwell, "Motor Function and the Hybridity of the American Negro" (4), which is very favorably regarded by Shuey (5) for having "employed painstaking techniques in classifying the Negro racial composition of the [subjects] into three groups." Codwell admitted that he utilized skin color determined according to the Von Luschan Color Scale as his basic criterion, but to this he added eye color, hair form, lip thickness, and nasal width. He was not much concerned with intelligence. As far as Codwell is concerned, his data show no significance on the point, despite Shuey's attempt to make this seem a major conclusion of his work. Instead, Codwell (6) was quite literally concerned with the "relationship of motor function to the hybridity of the American Negro" in order to "(a) contribute information about the relationship of motor function and the amount of 'Negroidness' of the American Negro, and (b) thus reveal the motor function significance of racial crossing." His major conclusion (7) was that "there is no significant change in the amount of motor function as a composite as the amount of Negroidness increases or decreases in the Negro-white hybird," although he did discover that his more Negroid subjects as a whole did better at something called the "Sargent Jump" and something else known as the "Burpee Test." Even this kind of conclusion is somewhat eroded by his penetrating observation (8) that "industry or effort is just as contributive to motor achievement as native endowment in motor skills."

The most useful studies linking race and certain specified socially valued traits or capacities make no pretense of dealing with biogenetic race, but admittedly work with categories of "social race." This is the case with the recent survey entitled *Equality of Educational Opportunity*, a publication of the National Center for Educational Statistics under the aegis of the Office of Education of the U. S. Department of Health, Education and Welfare (9). In an earlier version of this paper, I mistakenly criticized this excellent report for failing to define the racial categories it employs. Fortunately, Professor James S. Coleman (10), a principal author of that report, corrected me and pointed out that the "terms of identification" used in the report "are not used in the anthropological sense, but reflect social categories by which people in the United States identify themselves and identify others." Professor Coleman went on to say that "psychological reactions of a 'Negro' in American society to the fact of his being a Negro occur not as a result of the particular set of genes he possesses, but as a result of the fact that he is identified by others as a Negro, comes to identify himself as a Negro, is reacted to by others as a Negro, and believes himself a Negro."

This brings us to the very serious problem of delineating what people are. After all, doesn't everybody know white from Negro? Doesn't everybody know what he is? The question, though simply raised, is anything but simple. It raises serious problems of epistemology and cognition. Yet, without concerning ourselves with such matters in this brief session, we may still note a major division in handling concepts of racial identification. If *race* is to be treated as a sociocultural construct, it is very important to get the individual's views on his own identification and the identifications he applies to others. And, if race is to be treated as a biological construct, the lay individual's views of his own racial identity or that of anyone else is incompetent and immaterial. A scientific definition of race and of specifically designated racial groups should be based on specifiable metrical and morphological features capable of intersubjective identification. The use of "common-sense" categories is absolutely to be avoided. My colleague Marvin Harris (11) put it, "Common sense is completely unreliable in the matter of classification." Support for Harris's contention was recently published in *Science* (12).

Yet not long ago at the New York Academy of Sciences, I listened to a physical anthropologist discuss the relationship between dietary deprivation and intelligence differences between races. On the problem of racial identification, he stated that the impression of the eye was superior to the testimony of the calipers. To the credit of his audience, the point was received with some shock, and he was called to task in the question period. I am not agitating for a return to the cephalic index or similar eccentric indices of mysterious significance. But the calipers provide at least some basis for intersubjective identification, whereas the *coup d'oeil* is doomed to endless failure.

Now, for those who are trying to meet me halfway, only to be repelled by my apparent denial of incredibly obvious physical differences, let me clarify my position. I do not deny individual physical differences or do I deny that through time, at least up to now, these differences have tended to accumulate in statistically definable portions of the total human population.

I do maintain, however, that the species *Homo sapiens* is one continuum with all nodal points connected by intergrades. I believe, from what I know of fossil hominid populations, that this condition has persisted for half a million or more years, and the nodal points probably have varied through time. I believe that nodal extremes have been rendered less extreme during the past 10,000 years and especially during the past 500 years because of increased physical mobility and associated gene flow. Given the probability of increased numbers of individuals having internodal constellations of genotypes, it follows that correct racial typing becomes more and more difficult and demands full-scale attempts to control the genealogical histories of all subjects.

I also have strong convictions of the total inadequacy of common-sense racial typing, which are supported by studies of cognition in which respondents were shown pictures representing individuals of markedly different physical type (i.e., possessing different coloration, hair form and color, eye color, eyelid formation, nasal structure and size, etc.). Studies of this kind carried out in Brazil indicated (a) potential proliferation of racial categories to the extent of several hundred taxa, and (b) different identifications of the same individual by different respondents. In relation to point (b) observations made in Burma showed that individuals attributed different ethnic identities to themselves at different times for different social purposes. I submit that similar activities occur regularly in these United States in conjunction with so-called racial classification.

These are only a few of the reasons why I believe that any scientific study in which human race appears as a variable should be required to submit a careful and objective definition of race, an enumeration of the specific criteria applied to the sample population, and some proper control of the relationship of these criteria to the population in the light of population genetics. Assertions such as those by Garrett (13), Shuey, and others that "the American Negro constitutes a recognizable and clearly defined group; and the criterion of membership in this group is (more-or-less) African ancestry" are travesties of scientific statements.

As I wrote these remarks, two notions preyed on my mind. One was that few persons would find anything to disagree with in the general points I have been making. That is, apart from some of the details, I suspect that most educated people are willing and able to discriminate between serious, methodologically well-founded studies and those which I have labeled as pseudoscientific. And with this thought arose another: that all of this had occurred before, not once but several times, that Herskovits and Klineberg and other fine social scientists had passed this way before, often with more cogent and more elegant arguments than these now presented. I do not say that they failed in their intentions; certain ameliorations have occurred. But one thing they did not do is stop the nonsense. The pseudo studies go right on. What is more, some fine scientific journals throw open their pages to serious discussion of this nonsense. Those who oppose the pseudo study of race are called "equalitarians," and this term has been skillfully manipulated to make it appear as if there are two valid camps participating in a normal scientific exchange. But this is not a question of digging the "Mohole" or not, or whether *Homo habilis* is or is not an Australopithecus. It is more like dividing on the question of whether or not to exterminate six million Jews: one side says no and presents its arguments, and the other side says yes and presents its arguments, and this too becomes a debatable scientific question.

Participation in a debate over racial differences in intelligence, ability, or achievement potential is not a means of asserting and spreading knowledge of the views of professionally concerned scientists. Quite the opposite, it is a means of lifting in the public eye the status of studies that are otherwise disqualified and rejected by science. There is a need to stop the pseudoscientific investigation of race. There is even more need to end practices whereby such studies are treated as serious intellectual endeavors. If we recognize them for what they are, expressions of bias and propaganda tracts favoring certain social arrangements, it will be easier to confine them to the pages of such magazines as the *Mankind Quarterly*.

I do not mean to imply that there can be no scientifically valid studies of race. One bright group of young anthropologists is pushing in the direction of a "new new-physical-anthropology," which includes a more thorough blending of somatic studies, physiology, ethnology, and genetics. It is easy to tell the new-new school from the new school, because the latter is relatively at home with a symbol-based, superorganic concept of culture. The former, however, has aspirations toward the reduction of culture to species-specific behavior. Methodologically, this is accomplished by emphasizing feedback relations between phenotype and behavior; they include genetic structures while minimizing the significance of those parts of the total system which some of us would like to treat as cultural. This new approach is likely to spread a new biologism among young social scientists. That such an approach should emerge is not surprising to anyone who views intellectual developments as an essentially dialectical process. It is, at least in part, a reaction to the superorganicism, or at least the antireductionism, that has enjoyed a high, if not unchallenged, place for about two decades.

We may expect a growing number of technically expert, theoretically sophisticated studies of the interaction of somatic structures, genetic structures, and ethology. As a consequence of the proficient training of the new new-physical-anthropologists, we also may expect that most of their findings will be precise and will apply to small populations, well controlled for genetic information. In short, they should begin to meet the criteria for truly scientific studies of populations. But they will be studies of populations, not of races. Yet in the penumbra of these studies there will be a circle of intellectual jackals, eager to gain access to the results for uses never contemplated by the scientists who carried out the research. I will conclude, therefore, with a warning applied to my prophecy: scientists carrying out *bona fide* studies of populations have a further obligation to present their results in such fashion as to make difficult, if not impossible, their pseudoscientific application to race. Should such usage be attempted, the scientists who authored the original study must immediately reject and disown the false application.

Science has no social responsibilities, but scientists must accept social responsibility or face the consequences. Racial problems are as fraught with danger and potential disaster as problems of nuclear proliferation or of national rivalries in the exploration and use of outer space. It is now clear that the scientific study of individual subjects will have to conform to a code of standards that will protect the subject's health, security, and rights. What I am suggesting is only a slight extension of the element of social responsibility from the individual subject to the larger social aggregates whose futures are just as much influenced by this work.

NOTES AND REFERENCES

1. Audrey M. Shuey, *The Testing of Negro Intelligence* (Lynchburg, Va., J. P. Bell Co., 1958; 2nd ed., New York, Social Science Press,

1966). Unfortunately, a copy of the 1966 edition was not available to me, hence my comments pertain to the 1958 edition.

2. *Ibid.*, 3–4 (italics in the original).

3. *Ibid.*, 271.

4. John E. Codwell, "Motor Function and the Hybridity of the American Negro," *Journal of Negro Education,* 18 (1949), 452–64.

5. Shuey, *Negro Intelligence,* 280.

6. Codwell, "Motor Function," 453.

7. *Ibid.*, 463.

8. *Ibid.*, 460.

9. James S. Coleman et al., *Equality of Educational Opportunity* (Washington, Government Printing Office, 1966).

10. James S. Coleman, letter in *Columbia University Forum,* 10 (1967), 52–53.

11. Marvin Harris, *The Nature of Cultural Things* (New York, Random House, 1964), 10.

12. Brent Berlin, Dennis E. Breedlove, and Peter H. Raven, "Folk Taxonomies and Biological Classification," *Science,* 154 (1966), 273–75.

13. Henry E. Garrett, " 'Facts' and 'Interpretations' Regarding Race Differences," *Science,* 101 (1945), 404–6; cf. Shuey, *Negro Intelligence,* 4.

IRWIN KATZ

Some motivational determinants of racial differences in intellectual achievement

It is of considerable scientific and practical significance that in all regions of the United States the scholastic performance of Negro youth is, on the average, inferior to that of whites. The achievement gap has always existed, yet psychologists and educators lack precise under-standing of its causes. Until recently little research was done on the problem, and most of the few studies made were narrowly concerned with the measurement of racial differences in IQ scores. There is now emerging a more promising trend toward studies of cognitive and moti-vational processes in the development of children from different social backgrounds. This paper will examine the academic achievement of Negro students from the standpoint of some general concepts of motiva-tional processes underlying the development of intellectual achieve-ment behavior.

The basic facts about the public education of Negro Americans were assessed by Coleman et al. (1) in a nation-wide survey involving 645,000 pupils in over 4000 elementary and high schools. This report describes conditions that have long been known to educators from informal observations.

From the *International Journal of Psychology*, 2 (1967), 1–12. Reprinted by permission of the International Union of Psychological Science and DUNOD, 92 rue Bonaparte, Paris VI°. The preparation of this paper was supported by Contract N00014-67-A-0181-0004 between the Office of Naval Research and the University of Michigan. The author is the principal investigator.

1. On objective tests of scholastic achievement and ability the average scores of Negroes at every grade level that was studied are about one standard deviation below white norms. This means that about 85 per cent of the Negro school population test below white averages for the same grade level. The racial gap, when expressed in terms of Negro and white score distributions, remains fairly constant in the North throughout the school years, while in the South it grows progressively larger from grade 1 to grade 12.

2. In the North as well as the South, most Negro students (about 66 per cent for the entire nation) attend public schools with predominantly nonwhite enrollments.

3. Throughout the country the quality of educational services, including school curriculums and facilities and the verbal ability of teachers, available to minority group members is usually inferior to that enjoyed by whites in the same communities.

These facts provide the background against which to examine motivational aspects of Negro performance in the classroom. A number of general concepts for analyzing achievement striving have been advanced during the last few years.

THE ATKINSON MODEL OF ACHIEVEMENT MOTIVATION

Atkinson (2) has proposed a conceptual model of achievement motivation in which the strength of the impulse to strive for success on a given task is regarded as a joint function of the person's motive to achieve (measured as a personality characteristic), the subjective probability of success, and the incentive value of success. The notion of a motive to achieve, which grew out of McClelland's work on n Achievement (3), stresses a predisposition to experience gratification or its opposite in connection with self-evaluations of the quality of own performance. The incentive value of success is assumed by Atkinson to be equal to the apparent difficulty of the task, that is, to be an inverse function of the subjective probability of success. According to the model, on a task that has evaluative significance (e.g., a classroom test) motivation is maximal when the perceived probability of success is intermediate (i.e., is at the .50 level). One way in which the model has relevance for the study of minority-group students is with respect to the effect of variations in the race of teachers and classmates on the expectancy of success and the incentive value of success.

In a number of experiments my associates and I found that Negro male college students tended to underperform on intellectual tasks when whites were present. These studies were reviewed in an article (4) which also speculated that for Negroes who find themselves in predominantly white academic achievement situations, the incentive value of success is high but the expectancy of success is low because white standards of achievement are perceived as higher than own-race standards. By the same token, the perceived value of favorable evaluation by a white adult authority is high, but the expectancy of receiving it is low. Therefore, by experimentally controlling Negro subjects' expectancy of success on cognitive tasks it should be possible to produce the same, if not higher, levels of performance in white situations as in all-Negro situations.

Experiments have recently been carried out to test this line of reasoning. One study was done at a southern Negro college that has no admission criteria other than high school graduation. Most of the students had attended southern segregated public schools. Only a part of the experimental procedure and results need be described. Male freshmen were administered a digit-symbol task that was described as being part of a scholastic aptitude test. Their scores, they were told in advance, would be evaluated by comparison with the norms of certain other colleges, which they knew to have predominantly white student bodies. By means of false feedback about their scores on a previous practice trial of the same test, one third of the men were led to believe they had little chance of equaling the norm for their age group, one third were informed they had about an even chance, and one third were told they had a very good chance. Then half of the men in each probability-of-success condition were tested by a white person, and half were tested by a Negro. The results showed that in the low and intermediate probability conditions performance on the digit-symbol task was better with a Negro tester, but when the stated probability of achieving the white norm was high, the performance gap between the two tester groups closed. (Another finding of interest was that, in accordance with Atkinson's theory, highest performance with both Negro and white testers occurred in the intermediate probability condition.)

Another experiment, very similar to the previous one except that the task consisted of a series of simple arithmetic problems, was replicated on male undergraduates at two southern Negro colleges. One college has relatively high standards of admission that exclude the lower 50 per cent of the state's Negro high school graduates, while the other college admits all high school graduates, regardless of their academic standing. At both colleges, most students had attended southern segregated public schools. In Table 1 the results are presented. It can

TABLE 1

EFFECT OF RACE OF TESTER AND PROBABILITY OF SUCCESS ON ARITHMETIC GAIN SCORES (POST-PRE) OF MALE STUDENTS AT TWO SOUTHERN NEGRO COLLEGES[a]

	Probability of Success		
	Low	Medium	High
College A (Selective)			
White tester	1.4	1.7	2.4
Negro tester	.8	1.1	1.3
College B (Nonselective)			
White tester	.4	.3	1.9
Negro tester	2.1	2.5	1.9

[a] Significant main effects: College A, race of tester, $p < .05$, College B race of tester, $p < .005$. Significant interaction: College B, race $\times$ probability of success, $p = .05$.

be seen that at the nonselective college the effect of varying the race of the tester was essentially the same as in the previous study, which used a different task. When the probability of success was low or intermediate, higher scores were obtained by the Negro tester groups, but in the high probability condition there was no tester difference. For the selective college, however, scores were higher when the tester was white, regardless of the probability of success. (At neither college was there a significant tendency for scores to peak in the intermediate probability condition.) In summary, it appears that Negro students who had been average achievers in high school (the nonselective college sample) were discouraged at the prospect of being evaluated by a white person, except when they were made to believe that their chances of success were very good. But Negro students with a history of high academic achievement (the selective college sample) seemed to be stimulated by the challenge of white evaluation, regardless of the objective probability of success.

As yet, no studies of the type just described have been done on minority-group students below the college level. It would be worthwhile to investigate in actual classroom settings the dynamics of expectancy of success and incentive value of success as they are related to the race of the teacher and the race of the minority pupil's classmates. Indirect evidence from the Coleman survey tends to support my assumptions that *in predominantly white situations, the value of achievement is relatively high for the typical Negro student, while the expectancy of achievement tends to be low*. The survey found that in predominantly white, as compared with segregated Negro, schools in the North, the Negro pupils have *a stronger sense of opportunity* for meaningful achievement but *less confidence in their own ability*.

INTERNAL VERSUS EXTERNAL SOURCES OF EVALUATION AND REWARD

Crandall (5) has focused on the *development* of achieving behavior in young children. Unlike Atkinson, who is primarily concerned with the component of the incentive value of success that arises *internally*, from the feeling of pride of accomplishment, Crandall attaches major importance to an external source of incentive value, the approval of significant other persons. Corresponding to internal and external sources of incentive value, in Crandall's formulation, are two types of achievement standard. Children and adults who are primarily motivated in achievement areas by the desire for approval characteristically look to others to define the competence of their performance. Hence their standards mirror or reflect the standards or reactions of other persons and are designated *reflective achievement standards*. On the other hand, persons who are internally motivated to achieve are likely to evaluate their own efforts almost exclusively on the basis of their own subjective achievement standards, tending to ignore the criteria of others. Such individuals are said by Crandall to hold *autonomous achievement standards*.

Although Crandall does not elaborate this point, it is useful to think of the development of achieving behavior as a two-stage process. During the first stage, which begins as early as the second year of life in the white middle-class home, the child's efforts to acquire language and solve problems are reinforced by strong expressions of approval from parents or parent surrogates. If the approval is given frequently yet selectively in response to reasonable efforts at mastery in a variety of verbal and cognitive areas, the child will eventually develop strong habits of striving for proficiency. To be maintained, these habits must continue to be reinforced in a consistent manner. The second stage of development is reached when parents' standards and values of achievement are internalized by the child. The process may be described as one in which the child's own implicit verbal responses acquire, through repeated association with the overt responses of the parents, the same power to guide and reinforce the child's own achievement behaviors. That such verbal mediation processes occur in young children has been experimentally demonstrated by Russian psychologists in a series of ingenious conditioning experiments reported by Razran (6). In all likelihood, internalization does not take place until strong, externally reinforced, achieving habits have developed. But there may be a considerable amount of overlap of the two stages, so that older children, and even adults, may be impelled to achieve by both the desire for favorable self-evaluation and the desire for the approval of others. The relative strength of each motive will vary among individuals and, perhaps, depend upon the type of achievement situation. Thus, boys who are high achievers in high school have been found in a number of studies to be high on internal drive (n Achievement) and also docile, conforming, and anxious (7).

Unfortunately the evidence bearing on the role of social reinforcement in the early acquisition of achievement behaviors is both sparse and contradictory (7). The inconsistency in results is probably due to the research methods employed, most of the findings being based upon interviews (often retrospective) with parents and children, rather than direct observation of parent-child interaction. Even interviews with mothers of young children would not necessarily provide the relevant information about child behavior–maternal reinforcement contingencies, since the mother may not be fully aware of the extent to which her own responses and those of the child have mutually "shaped" one another. The few studies that have employed direct observation of parent-child interaction generally show a relationship between maternal approval and children's achievement striving. Crandall et al. (8) observed the behavior of white middle-class mothers and their preschool children in the home. Mothers who usually rewarded approval-seeking and achievement efforts had children who displayed more achieving behavior, both at home and in a nursery school free-play situation when the mother was not present. Other types of maternal behavior, such as reactions to children's help seeking and emotional support seeking, were not predictive of children's performance. Rosen and D'Andrade (9) took achievement tasks into the homes of boys who had very high or very low *n* Achievement scores, as measured projectively. Mothers of boys with strong *n* Achievement were more inclined to give approval when performance was good and to criticize incompetent efforts. Although these mothers, according to the investigators, were more likely to give their sons greater option as to exactly what to do, they gave less option about doing something and doing it well.

One may reasonably expect to find class and race differences in the extent to which parents reinforce language and problem-solving behavior. In low-income homes, where families tend to be large and mothers often work during the day, each child generally gets less individual attention from adults than do children in middle-class households. Also, because of their own educational deficiencies, it is often difficult for lower-class parents to know how to encourage intellectual behavior in their children or even how to recognize it when it occurs. The study of class and race differences in maternal behavior by means of direct observation has hardly been attempted as yet, except by Hess and Shipman (10) at the University of Chicago. In a pioneering study, they gave cognitive tasks to Negro mother-child pairs of different class backgrounds. Lower-class mothers gave their children less praise for problem-solving attempts and were less able to evaluate the quality of the child's responses.

The present assumption is that lower-class children (and this would include most Negro children), because they have received less parental approval for early intellectual efforts, *remain more dependent than middle-class children on social reinforcement when performing academic tasks.* Middle-class children, who are likely to receive consistent social reinforcement of cognitive behavior in the home, have begun

to internalize approval for success and standards of success by the time
they enter elementary school. Hence, children who have not been rewarded for intellectual efforts should tend to avoid intellectual achievement situations and to seek out more promising situations. But when
constrained from avoiding intellectual activity, as in the classroom, they
should display a *high need for approval,* as well as *performance standards that are highly reflective of the immediate social environment.*
Crandall and others (11) found that northern Negro elementary school
pupils scored higher than white pupils on a test of the need for approval
(patterned on the Crowne-Marlow Social Desirability Scale). Moreover, high scorers were likely to be shy, withdrawn, inhibited, and
lacking in self-confidence. There is also some evidence from other
studies, for example, one by Rosen (12), that lower-class Negro boys are
very low on n Achievement (which is here conceived as the capacity
for self-praise and autonomous standard setting). Mingione (13) found
lower-class Negro children to be inferior on n Achievement to white
children of low socioeconomic status.

The empirical evidence dealing with race and class differences
in children's responses to social reinforcement is meager and inconsist-
ent. Zigler and Kanzer (14) did an experiment in which two types of
verbal reinforcers, those emphasizing praise and those emphasizing correctness, were dispensed to white seven-year-old boys working at a simple
gamelike task. Words connoting praise ("good" and "fine") were more
effective reinforcers for lower-class children than words connoting correctness ("right" and "correct"). The reverse was true for middle-class
children. However, a similar study by Rosenhan and Greenwald (15)
did not bear out the findings. Neither class nor race differences were
observed in the relative effects of praise and correctness feedback on
children's performance of a simple conditioning task. More recently,
Rosenhan (16) obtained results that seem to contradict both earlier
experiments. White and Negro lower-class boys, as compared with
white middle-class boys, showed greater facilitation when told "right"
for correct responses, and greater decrements when told "wrong" for
incorrect responses, on a simple probability learning task.

Perhaps the inconclusiveness of the social reinforcement experiments can be attributed to a failure to control and manipulate certain
critical variables and to use appropriate tasks. None of the studies used
verbal-symbolic tasks of the sort that reveal race and class differences in

academic achievement, and none varied either the child's need for approval or the class-ethnic characteristics of the experimenter. The adult experimenter who dispensed rewards was always recognizably white middle-class. It is entirely possible that the visible social status of an adult authority strongly influences the socially disadvantaged child's interpretation of the adult's behavior.

Related to this point is evidence that Negro and lower-class children perceive their teachers as rejectant, and that the perceptions are to some extent veridical. Davidson and Lang (17) found that, regardless of pupils' achievement level in school, those from blue-collar homes attributed to their teachers less favorable feelings toward them than did children from more advantaged homes. In another study (18), Negro students in northern integrated high schools described their white teachers as disinterested and insincere. White middle-class teachers, it has been reported, do tend to underestimate the ability of minority children, misinterpret their goals, and express a preference for teaching white pupils (19, 20).

In a recent unpublished experiment my associates and I undertook to assess the extent to which the verbal learning of minority-group children from blue-collar homes is influenced by praise or blame from a Negro or a white adult in interaction with their need for approval. Northern urban Negro boys of elementary school age were individually administered a list of paired associates for ten trials. Subjects were assured at the outset that their performance would not affect their school grades. Half of the boys were tested by a Negro and half by a white person. Also, half of them received periodic approval from the experimenter ("I'm pleased with the way you're doing," etc.) and half received periodic disapproval ("I'm disappointed in the way you're doing," etc.). Finally, the sample was dichotomized into high and low on the need for approval, measured before the learning task was introduced by means of a modified version of the Crowne-Marlow scale. Each boy's learning score was expressed as an average deviation (positive or negative) from the median learning scores of the total sample on three blocks of trials.

There were two main effects: more learning occurred with Negro testers than with white testers, and more learning occurred when the tester gave approval than when he gave disapproval. But of greatest interest was an interaction of all three variables, the nature of which is revealed in Table 2. In order to account for the results, two types of assumptions will be made: (*a*) that the scale used to measure the need for approval actually tapped the subject's generalized predisposition to

TABLE 2

CELL MEANS FOR INTERACTION EFFECT OF NEED FOR APPROVAL, RACE OF TESTER, AND TESTER RESPONSE ON LEARNING SCORES (EXPRESSED AS DEVIATIONS FROM MEAN OF TOTAL SAMPLE) OF NEGRO BOYS[a]

	Negro Tester		*White Tester*	
	Approval	*Disapproval*	*Approval*	*Disapproval*
High need	2.41	1.42	1.24	−3.80
Low need	2.51	−1.33	−1.82	− .79

[a] All differences between cell means of 2.04 and greater are significant at the .05 level of probability by the Duncan test.

seek approval and avoid disapproval; and (*b*) that the Negro tester was perceived as predisposed to like the child and to react objectively to his performance, whereas the white tester was seen as inclined to dislike the child and to withhold genuine approval. The results shown in Table 2 can now be interpreted in the following manner. When the Negro tester was approving, all boys, regardless of need level, were adequately motivated for the task. When the Negro tester was disapproving, high-need boys were somewhat disheartened but continued to seek approval. (Their learning was somewhat poorer than in the Negro tester-approval condition, but not significantly so.) Low-need boys, on the other hand, tended to lose interest in the task, since it was defined at the outset as having no academic significance. When the tester was white and gave approval, high-need boys did not work quite as hard as boys who received approval from the Negro tester (difference nonsignificant). Though the white person's approval was seen as less genuine, their high need generated a moderate impulse to work (perhaps, in part, to avoid disapproval). Low-need boys were relatively unmotivated by white approval. When the white tester was disapproving, high-need children experienced debilitating anxiety, because the disapproval was taken as an overt expression of dislike; it was as though they could not hope to elicit a favorable response through greater expenditure of effort. These boys were virtually unable to learn at all. When low-need subjects were disapproved of by the white adult their performance did not deteriorate further. (The slight nonsignificant improvement in scores over the white tester-approval condition is inexplicable except as a sampling error.)

The experiment shows that in order to understand the effects of positive and negative social reinforcement on Negro children, it is necessary to take into account the need state of the individual child and the racial identity of the adult dispenser of reinforcement. Why the race of the tester influenced the verbal learning of northern urban Negro boys is not immediately apparent. Although the assumption that the subjects felt less rapport with white experimenters is a reasonable one, there is no direct evidence to support it. Indeed, even if the assumption is valid, it is entirely possible that a relatively brief experience of friendly interaction with the white adult would have changed the Negro child's responses in the learning situation. *Therefore, the results may have implications, not for biracial teacher-pupil pairs per se, but only for situations in which the Negro child perceives the white person as hostile, unfriendly, or disinterested.*

To summarize, it has been suggested as being of some significance that lower-class Negro children tend to be externally oriented in situations that demand performance; that is, they are likely to be highly dependent on the immediate environment for the setting of standards and dispensing of rewards. Some of the implications for educational practices are immediately apparent. First, teacher attitudes toward Negro children will be highly important for their classroom behavior. It has already been noted that attitudes of white teachers toward Negro pupils may generally be less than optimal. The evidence on this point is very sparse. (Even the Coleman survey did not adequately assess teacher attitudes toward minority-group pupils.)

Second, Negro students should be highly sensitive to the educational quality of both teacher and classmates, so that variations in these qualities should produce larger differences in the academic achievement of Negroes than of whites. The Coleman report (1) has data bearing upon this point. It was found that the achievement of both Negro and white pupils, when their family background characteristics were partialled out, was more closely related to the educational proficiency of their classmates than to all objective school characteristics together (i.e., curriculum, expenditure per pupil, physical facilities, size of class, etc.)

and to all teacher characteristics together. In the upper grades the apparent influence of the quality of the student body on individual achievement was two to three times greater for Negro pupils than for white pupils. The Coleman data represent correlations between variables, and causality must be inferred with utmost caution. Yet it seems a reasonable conclusion that a major part of the effect of the student body on individual achievement can be attributed to the high standards of performance set in the classroom. Teacher characteristics were almost as closely related to the Negro pupil's test scores as were student body characteristics. Teacher quality was much more important for Negro pupils than for white pupils. Beyond grade 1, Negroes were several times more sensitive to teacher variables than were whites. The most important characteristics of teachers were educational background and verbal ability.

Given the relatively high proficiency of white students and their teachers, it is not surprising that as the proportion of whites in a school increased, Negro achievement rose. The apparent impact of desegregation can be illustrated by comparing scores on reading comprehension for northern Negro high school students who never had a white classmate with scores of northern Negroes with similar family backgrounds who attended integrated schools from the early grades. When figures from Table 3.3.2 of the Coleman report are consolidated, it is revealed that Negro ninth graders with the longest experience of integrated schooling had an average score of 48.2. This is about five points below the white norm for the same region, but less than two points below the national norm of 50. In contrast, ninth-grade minority-group children who never had white classmates averaged 43.8. Thus it seems that desegregation reduced the racial achievement gap by almost half. (The Coleman report also gives scores of twelfth graders, which were excluded from the present comparisons because the high rate of Negro dropouts makes them unrepresentative. Actually, the picture would not have been changed materially by their inclusion.)

When the influence of the student body's educational background and aspirations is controlled, the relationship between racial composition of schools and Negro test scores is sharply reduced. Thus the apparent beneficial effect of having a high proportion of white classmates comes not from racial composition per se, but from the high educational quality that is, on the average, found among white students.

Desegregation also appeared to have the effect of increasing the variability of Negro test scores. The differences in variance were small but consistent, and accord with notions advanced earlier in this paper regarding the complex determination of Negro motivation in predominantly white settings: because of the high prestige of white teachers and age peers, rejection by them is more disturbing to the Negro pupil, and acceptance by them more facilitative, than similar responses from Negro teachers and peers. In addition, expectancy of success and value of success should tend to be affected in opposite ways by an increase in the proportion of white classmates, because of the elevation of achievement standards.

Further unpublished analyses of the Coleman data by James McPartland reveal the expected difference between truly *integrated* and merely *desegregated* schools. Those schools with student bodies more than half white, whose Negroes score well, when compared with similar schools whose Negroes score poorly, are characterized by greater cross-racial acceptance, as predicted. Their students were much more likely to report close friends among members of the other race than were students in the merely desegregated schools.

SENSE OF CONTROL OF REWARDS

Another valuable concept for understanding the educational achievement of children from different social backgrounds is Rotter's (21) *sense of personal control of the environment*. Individuals differ in the extent to which they feel that they can extract material and social benefits from the environment through their own efforts. In its broadest meaning, this construct refers to the degree to which people accept personal responsibility for what happens to them. It has been applied more specifically to children in intellectual achievement situations by means of a questionnaire that assesses the extent to which favorable reactions from parents, teachers, and peers are believed by the child to depend either upon the quality of his own efforts or upon extraneous factors, such as luck or the personal bias or whim of the evaluator (22). A child's feelings about whether his own efforts determine his external rewards clearly will affect his perception of the attractiveness or the *value* of a given achievement goal and his *expectancy* of success. The greater his need for approval in achievement situations, and the more his standards tend to be reflective, the closer will be these relationships. Crandall and others (22) found a tendency for sense of control and need for approval to be inversely related in white children.

A reciprocal causal relationship should exist between beliefs about locus of control and achievement, since these beliefs will affect task motivation, and the level of performance will in turn affect the rate at which the environment dispenses rewards. Thus Crandall and others (23) found that grade-school boys who felt they controlled their reinforcements earned high scores on intellectual tests and engaged in much intellectual free-play behavior. Similar results were obtained by Coleman and his coworkers. In this connection it is interesting to note that perception of internal control appears to be related to both white and middle-class status (1, 22, 24).

In the Coleman survey, three expressions of student attitude were measured: interest in school work, self-concept as regards ability, and sense of control of own fate. Of all the variables that were evaluated, including eight features of family background taken together and a much greater number of objective school characteristics taken together, these three attitudes showed the strongest relation to performance at all grade levels studied. For Negroes, perception of fate control was clearly the most important. (To assess it, students were asked to respond to three statements—"Good luck is more important than hard work for success," "Every time I try to get ahead something or somebody stops me," and "People like me don't have much chance to be successful in life".) With or without family background characteristics partialled out, sense of fate control accounted for about three times as much variance in the test scores of Negroes as of whites at the higher grade levels, in both the North and the South.

White proficiency was more closely related to self-concept than to control of environment. In the words of the Coleman report, "It appears that children from advantaged groups assume that the environment will respond if they are able enough to affect it; children from disadvantaged groups do not make this assumption, but in many cases assume that nothing they will do can affect the environment—it will give benefits or withhold them but not as a consequence of their own action" (25). The crucial role of this factor in determining level of performance is suggested by the finding that Negro pupils who answered "hard work" scored higher on a test of verbal ability than did white pupils who chose the "good luck" response.

Only a small fraction of the variance in fate control was accounted for by family background factors, and almost none of it by objective school characteristics. However, one variable is consistently related both to this attitude and to self-concept. As the proportion of white pupils in the school increased, the Negro child's sense of internal control increased, but his self-concept declined. It would appear that in integrated classrooms minority-group children were less confident of their ability to compete but were more aware of opportunity.

SUMMARY

Several motivational concepts have relevance to the problem of racial differences in intellectual achievement in the United States. Among these are Atkinson's model of achievement motivation, Crandall's distinctions between external and internal sources of achievement standards and achievement value, and Rotter's notion of the locus of control. The purpose of this paper has been to suggest how these formulations can be integrated to account for many of the facts known about the performance of minority-group students and to suggest fruitful directions for future research. Among the broad research topics mentioned were race and class differences in the process whereby early social reinforcement of verbal-symbolic behaviors becomes internalized, race and class differences in external and internal dependency as related to academic motivation, and the role of expectancy of success and value of success on academic motivation. All of these factors need to be considered in the context of uniracial and biracial performance situations, with particular attention being given to the distinction between the racially integrated classroom, in which the minority child experiences genuine acceptance, and the merely desegregated classroom, where the minority child feels unwelcome.

REFERENCES

1. James S. Coleman and staff, *Equality of Educational Opportunity* (Washington, Government Printing Office, 1966).

2. John W. Atkinson, *An Introduction to Motivation* (Princeton, N. J., D. Van Nostrand Co., 1964).

3. David C. McClelland, J. W. Atkinson, R. W. Clark, and E. L. Lowell, *The Achievement Motive* (New York, Appleton-Century-Crofts, 1953).

4. Irwin Katz, "Review of Evidence Relating to Effects of Desegregation on the Intellectual Performance of Negroes," *American Psychologist*, 19 (1964), 381–99.

5. Vaughn J. Crandall, Walter Katkovsky, and Anne Preston, "A Conceptual Formulation for Some Research on Children's Achievement Development," *Child Development*, 31 (1960), 787–97.

6. Gregory Razran, "Soviet Psychology and Psychophysiology," *Behavioral Science*, 4 (1959), 35–48.

7. Vaughn J. Crandall, "Achievement," *Yearbook of the National Society for the Study of Education*, 62 (1963), 416–59.

8. Vaughn J. Crandall, Anne Preston, and Alice Rabson, "Maternal Reactions and the Development of Independence and Achievement Behavior in Young Children," *Child Development*, 31 (1960), 243–51.

9. Bernard Rosen and R. C. D'Andrade, "The Psychological Origins of Achievement Motivation," *Sociometry*, 22 (1959), 185–218.

10. Robert D. Hess and Virginia C. Shipman, "Early Experience and the Socialization of Cognitive Modes in Children," *Child Development*, 36 (1965), 869–86.

11. Virginia C. Crandall, Vaughn J. Crandall, and Walter Katkovsky, "A Children's Social Desirability Questionnaire," *Journal of Consulting Psychology*, 29 (1965), 27–36.

12. Bernard C. Rosen, "Race, Ethnicity, and the Achievement Syndrome," *American Sociological Review*, 24 (1959), 47–60.

13. Ann Mingione, "Need for Achievement in Negro and White Children," *Journal of Consulting Psychology*, 29 (1965), 108–11.

14. Edward Zigler and Paul Kanzer, "The Effectiveness of Two Classes of Verbal Reinforcers on the Performance of Middle- and Lower-Class Children," *Journal of Personality*, 30 (1962), 157–63.

15. David Rosenhan and Jean A. Greenwald, "The Effects of Age, Sex, and Socioeconomic Class on Responsiveness to Two Classes of Verbal Reinforcement," *Journal of Personality*, 33 (1965), 108–21.

16. David Rosenhan, "Effects of Social Class and Race on Responsiveness to Approval and Disapproval," *Journal of Personality and Social Psychology*, 4 (1966), 253–59.

17. Helen H. Davidson and Gerhard Lang, "Children's Perceptions of

Their Teachers' Feelings Toward Them Related to Self-Perception, School Achievement and Behavior," *Journal of Experimental Education,* **29** (1960), 107–18.

18. D. Gottlieb, "Goal Aspirations and Goal Fulfillments: Differences Between Deprived and Affluent American Adolescents," unpublished paper, 1964.

19. D. Gottlieb, "Teaching and Students: The Views of Negro and White Teachers," unpublished paper, 1963.

20. Harlem Youth Opportunities Unlimited, Inc. (HARYOU), *Youth in the Ghetto* (New York, 1964).

21. J. Rotter, M. Seeman, and S. Liverant, "Internal vs. External Control of Reinforcement: A Major Variable in Behavior Theory," in N. F. Washburne, ed., *Decisions, Values and Groups* (London, Pergamon Press, 1962), II.

22. Virginia C. Crandall, Walter Katkovsky, and Vaughn J. Crandall, "Children's Beliefs in Their Own Control of Reinforcements in Intellectual-Academic Achievement Situations," *Child Development,* **36** (1965), 91–109.

23. Vaughn J. Crandall, Walter Katkovsky, and Anne Preston, "Motivational and Ability Determinants of Young Children's Intellectual Achievement Behaviors," *Child Development,* **33** (1962), 643–61.

24. Esther Battle and Julian Rotter, "Children's Feelings of Personal Control as Related to Social Class and Ethnic Group," *Journal of Personality,* **31** (1963), 482–90.

25. Coleman, *Equality,* 321.

English, they would be classed as Negro or as white, depending on
the particular observer's perception of physical and behavioral "racial"
cues.

Clearly, the popular racial typologies in America are not based
on any competent genetic studies. It is also evident that observable
phenotypical characteristics are often totally irrelevant in the assignment of individuals to the racial groups. There are Negroes who "can
pass for white"; there are whites who "could pass for Negroes."

The popular American conceptions about race contrast sharply
with those of contemporary Brazil, where descent plays a negligible
role in establishing racial identity. Marvin Harris (12) has shown that
full siblings whose phenotypes are markedly different are assigned to
different racial categories. Harris's studies also indicate that more than
forty racial categories are utilized in Brazil and that there are hundreds
of racial terms constructed of combinations of these. In addition, there
are alternative meanings for the same term, as well as a lack of con-
sensus concerning the assignment of any particular term to a given
individual (13). Moreover, Harris points out that there is "a high
frequency of passing out to other categories in conformity with the
achievement of socio-economic success" (12). Phenotypical attributes
such as skin color, hair form, and nose or mouth shape enter into
Brazilian racial classifications, but no combination of these variants is
predictive of the "race" to which a person will be assigned since socioeconomic position is one important determinant of racial status.

In Japan, skin color does not necessarily enter into popular
racial classifications. The Burakumin or "outcastes" are popularly believed to be racially distinct from ordinary Japanese. They were formerly termed Eta—a word written with the characters for "defilement
abundant"—and were officially emancipated in 1871 but remain a minority group set apart from other Japanese by low socioeconomic status
and by residential segregation.

The Eta are Japanese who descended from the lowest stratum
in a hierarchical social system which existed in the earliest known
period of Japanese history and was formalized by edict in the seventh
century A.D. (14). At that time, the Imperial House created two major
categories: the free and the base. Included in the latter category were
peasants, certain artisan guilds, and slaves. By the tenth century, most
of the formalized class distinctions had become meaningless; social dif-

ferences between the free and the unfree were no longer observable, and most of the base guilds were free.

It was during this period that Buddhism became accepted throughout Japan, and the Buddhist beliefs fused with indigenous Shinto beliefs concerning the avoidance of impurity. According to Donoghue (14):

> The syncretic religious concepts that evolved associated the taking of life with ritual impurity, and the guilds whose livelihood depended upon animal slaughtering were physically and morally isolated from the "legitimate" society. The outcastes became known as Eta.

The Eta formed small enclaves on the outskirts of towns and villages, where they were joined by other marginal social groups such as beggars, criminals, vagabonds, and entertainers.

In Japan, some theories on the history of the outcastes suggest that they originated from a people different from the ancestors of the socially acceptable Japanese. One theory holds that the outcastes are descendants of the aboriginal inhabitants of the Japanese isles. Another theory maintains that they are descendants of Korean war captives brought to Japan in the late sixteenth century; a third considers the Eta to be the offspring of Negritoes of the Philippines (15).

Most Western scholars regard the outcastes as physically identical to other Japanese. However, in the 1920s and 1930s a number of Japanese scholars described the Eta as a distinct race, and today many laymen still regard the outcastes as racially distinct from other Japanese. The outcastes' "distinctive racial heritage" is allegedly manifest in their behavior and appearance. Outcastes are popularly considered to be dirty; they are likened to hoodlums and gangsters. They are said to be afflicted with venereal diseases, tuberculosis, and leprosy (14). They are said to have one rib bone missing, to have distorted sexual organs, and to have defective excretory systems. Since they are animals, dirt does not stick to their feet when they walk barefooted (16).

The data on popular racial classifications current in the United States, in Brazil, and in Japan indicate that any expedient set of physical and/or behavioral attributes may be taken as the basis for such classifications. In these and other popular racial taxonomies, there often is a fusion and/or confusion of behavioral and physical attributes, leading to the perpetuation of the notion of the inheritance of cultural characteristics.

The assignment of individuals to the various racial categories recognized in different societies is often based on perceived behavioral differences rather than on demonstrable physical differences. Even where physical differences exist between the "races" delineated, laymen usually make no attempt to ascertain the biological significance of these differences! Moreover, the physical and behavioral attributes which are perceived as characteristic of a group are usually "explained" as being racial in origin.

Despite the recognition by many scholars that popular racial classifications should not serve as a basis for scientific discussions of human variation and related topics, many scientific studies are based on these classifications. Moreover, many scholars provide support for these nonscientific classifications by stating or implying that the popularly and/or politically defined "races" can be distinguished on the basis of biologically relevant criteria.

"Scientific" justification for the classification of the Eta as a race was provided by Kikuchi Sanya, whose book on the outcastes was written "from an anthropological point of view." Ninomiya (17) summarizes Kikuchi's thesis as follows:

> There are many peculiarities of the *Eta,* such as (*a*) practice of eating meat when the Japanese proper despise it; (*b*) reddish tinge in eye color; (*c*) prominence of the cheek-bone; (*d*) non-Mongolian type of the eyes; (*e*) dolichocephalic head; (*f*) shortness of stature; and (*g*) shortness of the neck.

In the 1930s, a professor of anthropology at Tokyo Imperial University also was of the opinion that "the *Eta* are not of the Mongolian type," although he did not "make this as a definite conclusion" (17).

It is hardly necessary to document the fact that many scholars in the United States conduct research and write books which imply that the "white race" and the "Negro race" are genetically defined entities. It will suffice to point out that virtually all scholars who write about "race and intelligence" assume that the "races" which they study are distinguished on the basis of biologically relevant criteria. So accepted is this fact that most scholars engaged in such research never consider it necessary to justify their assignment of individuals to this or that "race" (18).

Even when scholars in the biological sciences devise or utilize racial classifications, these are generally no more than refinements of typologies used by laymen. Scientific racial typologies are usually based on presumptions about or intuitions regarding the distribution of genetic characteristics. The manifest bases for these typologies are variations in arbitrarily chosen phenotypical characteristics. Yet it is well known that the relationship between genotype and phenotype is not simple and that the effects of the operation of environmental forces on the phenotype are not genetically transmitted. Moreover, even when scientists make a serious attempt to base their racial typologies on genetic variants, they do not squarely face the problem that there should be some biologically relevant justification for the choice of the characters on whose variation the "races" are defined (19).

It cannot be expected that the difficulties inherent in the construction of racial classifications will be appreciated by laymen when these problems are not often acknowledged by the scientists themselves. Normally, the layman who reads the literature on race and racial groupings is justified in assuming that the existent typologies have been derived through the application of theories and methods current in disciplines concerned with the biological study of human variation. Since the scientific racial classifications which a layman finds in the literature are not too different from popular ones, he can be expected to feel justified in the maintenance of his views on race.

It is not surprising, therefore, that scientific discourses on race serve to buttress the popular belief that discrete racial groups exist among mankind or that scientific racial typologies serve to legitimize popular racial classifications. On the one hand, scientists often base their studies of "racial differences" on popularly and/or politically defined races. On the other hand, they often take popular racial classifications as a point of departure for the construction of their own typologies, which, on close examination, appear just as spurious as those utilized by laymen (20).

III

The literature on racial typologies of earlier historical periods in America further indicates that both scientific and popular racial classifications reflect prevailing sociopolitical conditions. Significant changes in the political status of some ethnic groups in America have led to reappraisals of their "racial" statuses and of the "racial" characteristics by which they were defined.

In contemporary America, there are a number of populations of European origin who comprise the "white race." Even though some laymen subdivide this race on the basis of the national origin or religious affiliation, most Americans agree that there is essentially one "white race." That scientists concur in this opinion is illustrated by the fact that no present-day study that proposes to compare races would compare Americans who came from Ireland with those who came from England. But this was not always the case. Barbara Solomon's book, *Ancestors and Immigrants* (21), which deals with racial ideologies in New England between the 1850s and 1920s, demonstrates that "white" people who are now regarded as members of one "race" were formerly divided into several "races." In the second half of the nineteenth century and the early decades of the twentieth century, various American scholars published works which divided and redivided peoples now termed white or Caucasian into the following "races": Anglo-Saxons, Celts, Teutons, Jews, and southern Europeans or "brownish races." Scandinavians were regarded as a branch of the Teutonic "race," and Teutons and Anglo-Saxons were regarded as cousins, "racially" speaking.

Between the 1830s and 1870s the industrial expansion of New England brought waves of immigrants from Europe to Boston and the surrounding areas. Most were from Ireland. In the early phases of immigration, the self-styled Brahmins, who comprised the New England aristocracy, decried the "racial inferiority" of these Irish immigrants. In the 1840s and 1850s many prominent New Englanders shared C. E. Norton's apprehensions about the "sudden influx of people so long misgoverned . . . [and] of a race foreign to our own" (22). Charles F. Adams, Jr. remarked that "the Irish race," being "quick of

impulse, sympathetic, ignorant, and credulous . . . have as few elements in common with native New Englanders as one race of men
well can have with another" (23).

By the 1870s, the Irish, representative of the so-called Celtic
race, gained dominance in some service industries in Boston and nearby
mill towns; by the 1880s, they wrested the political leadership of Boston from the old New England aristocracy. The political supremacy
of the Brahmins having been challenged, various academicians from
this aristocracy sought to prove that the increased influx of members
of the Celtic and other "inferior races" undermined the chances for
the survival of democratic institutions which were Teutonic in origin
and transmitted "through the blood."

During the 1870s, Francis A. Walker, a noted social scientist
who was to become a university president, was a leading spokesman
for those who were alarmed by the rising power of the alien Celts.
The census of 1880 confirmed Walker's suspicions that the birth rate
among the urbanized immigrant populations was exceeding that of the
native Anglo-Saxons, and he became obsessed by the "fecundity of the
foreign elements in the United States." During the 1880s Walker
wrote many articles on the evils of immigration and used his academic
affiliations to appeal to younger scholars to support his thesis that the
arrival of foreigners in the United States had caused a "shock to the
principle of population among the native element." By the end of the
1880s, "the happy ideal of assimilation, which [John] Fiske had spread
over the land, disintegrated under Walker's cogent proofs, and, for old
New Englanders, immigration became a matter of racial preservation"
(24).

Support for New England raciology had come from academic
circles in Europe. During the latter half of the nineteenth century one
of the most influential books was *The Races of Men*, written in 1850
by Robert Knox, a professor of anatomy at the Edinburgh College of
Surgeons, which proclaimed that all of civilization depended on race.
To the Celts, Knox attributed the following characteristics: "furious
fanaticism; a love of war and disorder; a hatred for order and patient
industry; no accumulative habits; restless, treacherous, uncertain; [one
need only] look at Ireland" (25). Knox saw the American Know-
Nothing riots as a prelude to the inevitable conflict between Saxons
and Celts. He said that "the war of race will some day shake the Un-

ion to its foundation. They never will mix—never commingle and unite" (25).

Edward A. Freeman, an Oxford historian, was another scholar who favored racial explanations of history. In 1881 when Freeman made a lecture tour of the United States, he proposed that "the best remedy for whatever is amiss in America would be if every Irishman should kill a Negro and be hanged for it" (26).

During the late nineteenth and early twentieth centuries, the appeals to limit European immigration were increasingly based on racial as well as economic arguments. The Immigration Restriction League of Boston, founded in 1894, was in the forefront of the battle to ensure that the Anglo-Saxon-Teutonic racial strains would not be overwhelmed by "Slav, Latin, and Asiatic races, historically down-trodden, atavistic, and stagnant" (27).

Solomon points out that historians, economists, sociologists, and physical scientists synthesized the earlier diffuse Teutonist sentiments into a pseudoscientific ideology of racial superiority. These academicians were influenced by the League's opinions; in turn, Brahmin restrictionist views were reinforced by the scholars' presentations. The Eugenics movement, which crystallized in America in the early twentieth century, argued that the influx of alien races had increased the rate of "insanity, imbecility, and feeblemindedness" in the population of the United States.

By the early twentieth century, however, less attention was being paid to the inferiority of the Celts than to that of the southeastern Europeans, who, according to the Eugenicists, "had hereditary passions which were unalterable, regardless of public schools and economic opportunities in the United States" (28). Restrictions on the immigration of these undesirables would be the initial step in the creation of a race of supermen in America.

The Anglo-Saxon, Teutonic, southern European, Jewish, and other "races" defined during this period of American history were considered immutable; the characteristics which distinguished them were endowed by heredity. As might be predicted, these "racial" characteristics were as often behavioral as physical. Despite the alleged immutability of these "races" and of the characteristics attributed to them, New Englanders did in fact change their evaluation of the so-called "races of Europe."

Between the 1830s and 1890s, the Celts were described as ignorant, shiftless, credulous, impulsive, and mechanically inept; they
were inclined toward drinking and related crimes. By the 1890s, when
the Irish were the political leaders of the hub of New England and
large numbers of southern Europeans were coming to the United States,
the Irish had become tolerated aliens. The shift in attitude toward the
Celtic race reflected the change in the political situation. The Irish
were said to have "a remarkable race trait of adaptability which explained the achievement of the more intelligent and prosperous of the
Boston group." Moreover, the Irish "above all races [had] the mixture
of ingenuity, firmness, human sympathy, comradeship, and daring that
[made them] the amalgamator of races" (29).

That there were no proven biologically significant differences
among the "races of Europe" did not prevent New Englanders from
perceiving European immigrant populations as separate races. So-called
racial differences were said to be manifest in life-styles; racial affiliation
could be determined by listening to individuals speak or by hearing
their names. In any case, even without perceptible clues, the relative
backwardness of the immigrants was "proof" of their inferior intellectual capabilities and characters, both of which were reputedly determined by "racial" heritage.

IV

Solomon's *Ancestors and Immigrants*, Gossett's *Race: The History of an Idea in America*, Stanton's *The Leopard's Spots* (30), and
Curtin's *Image of Africa* (31) provide abundant documentation for the
statement that at various historical periods, racial typologies and/or
ideologies have reflected prevailing sociopolitical conditions. Historically, both scientific and lay concepts of race have served to support
the economic and political privileges of ruling groups who regarded
themselves as superior by virtue of phylogenetic heritage rather than
because of the accidents of culture history.

From the preceding discussion it should be apparent that popular racial classifications are based on a wide range of emotional, political, and other evaluative criteria that are not relevant to the biological
study of human variation. The differences in popular racial typologies

become apparent when one shifts in time or place from one society to another. Therefore, it is obvious that there can be no justification for the elevation of any popular racial classification to the status of an analytic system in science.

Studies which purport to demonstrate the genetic basis for this or that behavioral characteristic observed among persons who make up popularly defined races are essentially nonscientific and should be labeled as such. Hence, to presume to study the genetic basis for some behavioral attribute of the "Negro race" in America is to ignore the fundamental difficulty of defining that "race." It is entirely probable that any biogenetically significant division of Americans would include some groups comprised of *both* so-called Negroes and so-called whites. But to isolate such groups would violate the folk theory that there is a pure white race and a Negro race which includes some so-called racial hybrids.

In conclusion, it must be made clear that this paper is not aimed at the deprecation of the study of human variation. The directions for future research into the genetics of human variation have been indicated by various writers, including the contributors to the volume entitled *The Concept of Race,* edited by Ashley Montagu. The isolation of those genetic characters that constitute the most variable array of features in mankind, the determination of the characters that admit of biologically significant clusterings of breeding populations, the study of the relationship between genotype and phenotype, including the investigation of genetic characters as they are represented in different life stages of individuals—these are some of the problems which have to be pursued.

These problems can and should be studied without reference to race, which has never been and never will be a primarily biological concept. The history of the use of the race concept by scientists and laymen alike makes it apparent that race could probably never be accepted as a purely statistical concept. Race is a biopolitical concept, the continued use of which will serve only to obfuscate the problems entailed in the study of human variation. As Livingstone (32) has pointed out:

> Just as Galileo's measurements and experiments paved the way for Newton's laws of motion, which totally replaced the Aris-

totelian laws of motion concerned as they were with describing
the nature of bodies and their "essences," our newer genetic
knowledge and the measurement of gene frequencies will replace
the studies on the nature or essence of race and the mathematical theory of population genetics will replace the Linnaean system of nomenclature.

NOTES AND REFERENCES

1. This is the position taken by a number of contributors to this sym-
posium. It is exemplified by Theodosius Dobzhansky in *Mankind
Evolving* (New Haven, Yale University Press, 1965), 266–69. It
also appears to be the view of William Boyd, *Genetics and the
Races of Man* (Boston, Little, Brown and Co., 1950), and of C. S.
Coon, S. M. Garn, and J. B. Birdsell in *Races* (Springfield, Ill.,
C. C Thomas, Publisher, 1950).

2. This point of view is represented by a number of contributors to
the volume *The Concept of Race,* edited by Ashley Montagu (New
York, The Free Press, 1964). For a critical examination of the
theoretical and methodological problems involved in racial classifications, see especially the articles by Jean Hiernaux, "The Concept
of Race and the Taxonomy of Mankind," 29–45; Frank B. Livingstone, "On the Nonexistence of Human Races," 46–60; Paul R.
Ehrlich and Richard W. Holm, "A Biological View of Race," 153–
79; and Nigel A. Barnicot, "Taxonomy and Variation in Modern
Man," 180–227.

3. Hiernaux, in *The Concept of Race,* 40.

4. See, for example, S. L. Washburn, "The Study of Race," in *The
Concept of Race,* 242–60.

5. Ehrlich and Holm, in *The Concept of Race,* 175; see also 154–55,
161–62, and 177–78.

6. Hiernaux, in *The Concept of Race,* 41–42.

7. N. W. Gillham, "Geographic Variation and the Subspecies Concept
in Butterflies," *Systematic Zoology,* 5 (1956), 110–20, quoted Ehrlich and Holm, in *The Concept of Race,* 167.

8. Livingstone, in *The Concept of Race,* 56.

9. See Thomas F. Gossett, *Race: The History of an Idea in America*
(Dallas, Southern Methodist University Press, 1963), 37–39, 69–70,
and 80.

10. *New York Times*, October 20, 1966, p. 21, reported that "Chinese-American public school children in Boston have been officially declared white by the School Committee ['the official city agency in charge of Boston's public schools'] in the latest phase of the controversy over racial imbalance in schools." One week later, it was reported that the Massachusetts State Board of Education had rejected the ruling of the Boston School Committee, and that Chinese-American children who had been classed as white would be reclassified as nonwhite. *New York Times*, October 27, 1966, p. 40.

11. Marvin Harris, *Patterns of Race in the Americas* (New York, Walker and Co., 1964), 56.

12. Marvin Harris, "Race," in *International Encyclopedia of the Social Sciences* (forthcoming edition).

13. Marvin Harris and Ruth Martinez, "Referential Ambiguity in the Calculus of Brazilian Racial Identity," unpublished manuscript.

14. This account of the history of the Eta is based upon John Donoghue, "An Eta Community in Japan: The Social Persistence of Outcaste Groups," *American Anthropologist*, 59 (1957), 1000–17. For additional data on this group, see George DeVos and Hiroshi Wagatsuma, eds., *Japan's Invisible Race: Caste in Culture and Personality* (Berkeley, The University of California Press, 1966).

15. See Shigeaki Ninomiya, "An Inquiry Concerning the Origin, Development, and Present Situation of the *Eta* in Relation to the History of Social Classes in Japan," *Transactions of the Asiatic Society of Japan*, Second series, Vol. 10 (1933), 47–154.

16. Kikuchi Sanya, *Eta-Zoku ni Kansuru Kenkyù* (A Study Concerning the *Eta* Race, Tokyo, 1923), cited in Ninomiya, *An Inquiry*, 56.

17. Ninomiya, *An Inquiry*, 56.

18. This is exemplified by the comments of Audrey M. Shuey in her book, *The Testing of Negro Intelligence* (Lynchburg, Va., J. P. Bell Co., 1958), and by comments of the authors whose studies are reviewed by Shuey.

19. For a discussion of the methodological problems involved here, see Hiernaux, 30–40 and Ehrlich and Holm, 160–61 and 163–64 in *The Concept of Race*.

20. For a sample of scientific racial typologies, see those summarized in Dobzhansky, *Mankind Evolving*, 256–66.

21. Barbara Solomon, *Ancestors and Immigrants* (Cambridge, Harvard University Press, 1956).

22. Charles Eliot Norton, "Goldwin Smith," *North American Review*, 205 (1864), 536, quoted in Solomon, *Ancestors*, 12.

23. Charles Francis Adams, *Three Episodes of Massachusetts History* (Boston, Houghton Mifflin and Co., 1892), Vol. II, 957, quoted in Solomon, *Ancestors,* 29.
24. Solomon, *Ancestors,* 69–79.
25. Robert Knox, *The Races of Men* (Philadelphia, 1850), 26–27 and 177, quoted in Gossett, *Race,* 96.
26. Edward A. Freeman, *Lectures to American Audiences* (Philadelphia, 1882), quoted in Gossett, *Race,* 109.
27. Solomon, *Ancestors,* 111.
28. *Ibid.,* 151.
29. *Ibid.,* 154.
30. William Stanton, *The Leopard's Spots* (Chicago, University of Chicago Press, 1960).
31. Philip D. Curtin, *The Image of Africa* (Madison, University of Wisconsin Press, 1964).
32. Livingstone, in *The Concept of Race,* 55.

THEODOSIUS DOBZHANSKY

Discussion

Let's be optimists. Let's be optimists and believe that conflicting opinions will help to bring forth truth. I'm an old compromiser, but the conflicting opinions expressed at this session are, I fear, beyond my ability to compromise. Let me, however, try.

Professor Fried suggests that we should end the pseudoscientific investigation of race. I do not think there is a single person in this audience who would wish to make pseudoscientific investigations of race or of anything whatever.

Professor Ingle has argued very cogently that the data are insufficient to assert that under similar environments, different human populations would exhibit equal potentialities. I submit that the elementary rule of genetics is that equal or unequal potentialities cannot be judged unless similar environments are provided. Hence, it is quite unreasonable to argue that we must first find that potentialities are equal and then provide similar environments. We must do the reverse.

Finally, in all such discussions, it is not the question of the average performance of this or that race which really matters; what matters is the variability within races or within any human group. The evidence clearly shows that there exist variants—persons within each human group who possess potentialities for cultural or intellectual development equal to or greater than the average potentialities for any other group. I think that this evidence is cogent and very important.

Professor Fried has correctly pointed out that there is no careful and objective definition of race that would permit delimitation of races as exact, nonoverlapping, discrete entities. Indeed, such criteria do not exist because if they did, we would not have races, we would have distinct species.

165

To deny the existence of racial differences within the human species is futile. This futility has been neatly demonstrated at our symposium. I find it amusing that those who questioned the validity of racial classifications have themselves used the word "race," or the term "so-called race," many times. Indeed, how else could they speak about human variation at all! The reliability and the usefulness of racial classifications have often been exaggerated. I agree that nothing good can be expected from badly planned and poorly executed race studies. I submit, however, that failure to use modern methods for scientific race studies is not a reasonable policy either. If scientists refuse to study races, we shall have pseudoscientific "studies" of races by race bigots. I feel that this would be a tragic mistake on the part of scientists. Let us not make this mistake!

JERRY HIRSCH

Discussion

Much of what I might say about the first paper was actually said in my own paper, presented at Session I. Dr. Ingle has spoken to us about the social and psychological aspects of the race construct, the social relevance of race classification, actually. He has suggested that we attend to individuality, and yet he has recommended that we make studies of average group differences.

Dr. Fried has argued that we have a need to end pseudoscientific investigation of race; he has given in considerable detail many of the criticisms of the present use of race in what he calls pseudoscientific studies. I was interested to note that many of the ways recounted by Dr. Marshall in which race is utilized as a folk concept were not very far different from several of the pseudoscientific uses of race Dr. Fried alluded to.

Dr. Katz paid very little attention to race per se; he gave us a discussion of techniques or approaches to the study of group differences in achievement. The differences he referred to, of course, were differences between groups from different races.

I think that one of the key points to be gleaned from these discussions at both this session and earlier ones is that it is a platitude that heredity and environment interact. If we take the population approach to questions of group differences and the study of behavior rather than the typological approach, we immediately come to realize that we cannot generalize about the role of genetics in behavior.

We should pay considerable attention to what Dr. Ingle recommended at the beginning of his talk, namely, to the individuality of the people we may want to acculturate, and that most of these dealings are going to have to be done on an *ad hoc* basis. We are going to have

167

to deal with individual people and try to fit them into what they desire
as niches in our culture.

I believe that it is very important for us to take an evolutionary
point of view—not evolutionary in the sense of hierarchy, either of
species or of races, but rather to think in terms of both biological
and social evolution. However we may wish to categorize the human
groups that we see today, we must remember that no matter what the
genetic evidence is for difference, there is also a very strong cultural
difference; what we have had is a biosocial evolution, and what we
have to concentrate our attention on today is the direction that we wish
our biosocial evolution to take in the future. I do not advocate a eugenics movement wherein on the basis of some average measurement,
we recommend that a particular people be allowed to breed and others
not, as Hitler did. But we can, where we have specific bits of information, such as we have in the trisomy case called Mongolism and in the
PKU case, recommend to people that they might not wish to breed.
This, I think, is as far as we can push genetic knowledge in its social
application today. Negative eugenics of this kind is being practiced in
clinics all over the country today; people are being told what the prob-
abilities are of their having children of one kind or another.

MARGARET MEAD

Concluding remarks

These papers have provided us with some material with which to approach the question of how present biological knowledge can be articulated with problems that confront the United States and the world. As long as genetic markers—pigmentation, hair form, facial configuration—are used to identify, stigmatize, or glorify certain portions of the population in ways that give them differential access to education, to economic resources, and to deference, the biological knowledge of the inheritance and significance of such characteristics will be socially and politically important. Wherever actual or imputed physical characteristics have functioned to erect barriers between groups and where these barriers are reinforced for individuals by the presence or absence of members of their own or other groups, a knowledge of the effects of early environment and experience also will be important.

Where—owing to various patterns of mating, voluntary or involuntary migration, and environmental factors—any portion of the population has been reduced in performance below its potentiality, the promise that Ginsburg and Laughlin hold out for the reemergence of a potential within that group as good and as varied as that of the currently most productive group in the world is highly significant. Assortative matings make it possible, once particular traits or talents become valued, for any population to reassemble potentials which have existed within the gene pool unrecognized. For example, where mathematical ability gives neither recognition nor reward, their hypotheses suggest that a man with such ability would have no special advantage for marriage with an individually gifted woman. But once such an ability becomes valued, the mathematically gifted man would not only be rewarded but also given an opportunity to marry a woman with specially valued abilities. Another example of such assortative mating is the existence of quasi-caste groups within societies where musicians marry into musicians' families or seamen into seamen's families.

There are many kinds of assortative matings that go on within complex societies; for example, it may be permissible for men of a dominant group to mate with women of a subordinate group but the reverse be discouraged. This may result in such anomalies as a greater frequency of marriages in which Negro men marry white women over marriages in which white men marry Negro women simply because white men can consummate such unions without legal formalities. One set of children will be reared as legitimate, the other as illegitimate; one will have access to white styles of behavior, one will not. The differences in later performance may be enormous, but they will not be genetic.

Another type of assortative mating was described by Herskovits (1) in the 1920s in which within the Negro group a light skin was so valued that light women preferred to marry darker men so as to have more enthusiastic economic support, and light men married darker women for the same reason. Warner and coworkers (2) have discussed the extent to which the lighter-skinned child was preferred and given a better education. Such selection operates independently of innate ability or the kind of assortative mating of which Ginsburg and Laughlin speak. When the innate abilities of members of disadvantaged groups are given recognition and when they are given equal opportunity to obtain education, many more talented and competent individuals may be expected to emerge from national, class, and caste groups that have not previously exhibited such capacities.

The experiments by Kilham and Klopfer show that with two types of chicks, yellow and black, there was no preference for own or alien strain if the chicks were reared without social experience, but that given social experience of own-kind, the preference for own-kind persisted; given experience of both kinds, there was a preference for own-kind; and that a complementary possibility, that chicks reared with an alien strain would develop a preference for the alien strain did not occur. Where we are assured that within the gene pool of a group of say 30,000 lie all the potentialities for special abilities, Kilham and Klopfer raise the question as to whether certain kinds of preference may be immanent in a genetic strain but require specific environmental conditions to activate them.

The classic case of Tryon's rats, cited so frequently throughout this symposium, highlights the dangers of premature dependence upon experiments in which the hierarchy of sensory cues has not been fully explored. Tryon bred for bright and dull rats from the same genetic strain by selecting those he bred according to their performance on special mazes. Success at running the mazes was dependent upon non-visual cues, however, and later experimenters reversed Tryon's results so that the bright rats performed as dull rats and the dull as bright when visual cues were essential to success in maze-running.

In a similar way, our school system may be seen as a kind of complex maze in which special types of early learning and early expectation of success in such learning tend to lead to success. So the reported discrepancies between children classified as Negroes and children classified as whites, with other factors such as age, sex, and social class held constant, simply provide us with a large amount of possibly significant evidence on the effects of racial classification on the kind of performance that is rewarded in our school system. This view of the school system is reinforced by the curious finding that there are fewer of those who must be classified as mentally retarded among the age group that has left school than there were in the previous year's school population. Successful adjustment in the real world does not draw only on such specialized abilities or such specialized early experiences as are necessary for success in the school system.

As Dr. Gordon pointed out, our present school system is not designed to evoke the same kind of behavior from children with sharply contrasting backgrounds, and projects like Head Start are necessary to test ways of compensating for preschool experience that is negatively related to school success. This, however, only deals with half of the problem; much more delicate work will need to be done to explore the possibility that our schools fail to evoke capabilities that children from differently organized homes may have developed during their preschool years. The present emphasis on bettering the conditions born of social discrimination, countered chiefly at present by sentimental objections to making lower-class children middle class, obscures the possibility that the kinds of concrete sensory responses engendered by an intimate, nonliterate environment within a larger society that over-values literacy may well have definite advantages, which to date have been manifested principally in the arts.

The significance of positive or negative feelings about physique was not mentioned in this symposium but is of increasing importance in today's world. Where there is conspicuous subordination of a social group on the basis of real or attributed physical features, and the rule of hypodescent prevails, the members of the subordinated group may repudiate their own physical characteristics and even penalize those individuals who manifest the disapproved characteristics to the most marked degree. The concept of Negritude in Africa is an example of a vigorous attempt to reassert the primacy, for any given group, of its own physical type. We must recognize the rising demand for the kind of world in which people can enjoy the way they look, be proud of the way their parents looked, and anticipate with pleasure the way their children will look. This is the kind of world in which diversity will be appreciated and in which the freedom of individuals to value their own physique and to move among and marry individuals of other physiques is not impaired at any point.

One of the most crucial problems of culture change is the capacity of groups or whole societies to adapt to change. It has been frequently demonstrated that a member of any group can approximate the behavior of the members of another group if removed as a child from his own group and educated in the other. The sons of African tribal chiefs educated in England are cases in point. Yet, the more far-reaching question is the extent to which a group with a given culture, especially when that culture is completely associated with a highly identifiable physique, can advance as a group and take on patterns of thinking and acting appropriate to the modern world. New Guinea tribes of comparable levels of culture but with markedly different methods of early childhood training have displayed very different histories of response to contact with more advanced cultures. Just as many of the specific handicaps of deprived groups that we once thought of as genetic have been successfully traced to malnutrition and specific maternal disease and not to heredity, so too other specific handicaps and failures to make previously untapped capacities manifest may be due to early childhood experience. The temporary advantages or political preponderance of one tribal group in a new nation over another, as in Nigeria or Indonesia, may be likewise attributable to the repercussions in early childhood of differences in historical experience.

Katz's experiments are just the beginning of a sophistication in human experiments to match the exquisite sophistication that has been attained in some of our comparative animal studies. Perhaps here, in the painstaking isolation of factors within a dynamic system, lies the strongest hope for understanding at least some of the factors in the different performances of human groups, differentiated by race, class, religion, or nationality.

Several speakers have emphasized the importance of substituting thinking about populations for thinking about typologies. This shift will, I believe, require considerable translation before it becomes part of the repertoire of lay thinking. Typologies assume genetic isolates in which all members of the given group display the same characteristics to the same extent. A layman may take the kind of distinction that can be made between a Hottentot without foreign mixture and a member of an isolated Eskimo group and apply it to differences between portions of populations long in contact. Thus, thinking typologically, the layman conjures up an image of "Negro" or "white man" and measures persons so classified as deviations from the ideal type—lighter or darker, hairier or less hairy than expected.

An isolated Eskimo with no biological mixture for twenty or thirty generations will be identifiable in many ways that make the construction of a type—with a range in many features—possible. Consider, however, what you know if an individual is characterized as a "Baltimore Negro," a member of a group whose blood groups indicate that they average 70 per cent African descent as Dr. Glass reported. What would you be able to predict about him? His pigmentation? No, for he might be fairer than many Mediterranean people. His features? No, they might run from features that he shared with some West African tribe to features that might identify him, incorrectly, as from India. His speech? Yes; he could be predicted to speak some form of English, but it might be a rural southern dialect, unintelligible to a speaker of standard English, or it might be marked by a Harvard accent or a California accent or British West Indian accent. Such an exercise highlights the fact that we have placed some members of our population in a special category because of some single trait or cluster of physical traits, known ancestors with such traits, or continuous self-attribution of Negro membership, when actually they should be thought of simply as part of the population of the United States. Negro Americans do constitute a partial Mendelian population because of preferential mating with one another, but this is enormously different from the state of an isolated group of Eskimo, African desert dwellers, or inhabitants of isolated Pacific islands.

At the same time, we are up against a rather serious dilemma today in the United States and to some extent in the world. We have groups of people classified as Negroes, Mexicans, and Amerindians who have been placed in a position of imputed inferiority and have often come to accept it themselves. Earlier the same thing happened to groups of immigrants from southern and eastern Europe who had imputed "racial" characteristics which influenced their learning capacities and potential for achievement. The 1921 Emergency Quota Act reflected this set of racial stereotypes. The immigrant groups gradually advanced in the United States as their children obtained an American education and they themselves obtained political and economic power. In developing a strategy to improve the condition of Americans of mixed racial background we are up against a rather more complicated problem.

The anti-integrationists cite the greater success of immigrants from self-consciously high cultures—the Japanese, the Chinese, and the Jews—who in spite of prejudice have demonstrated as high and often higher achievement levels than the older Americans. And certain leaders in the civil rights movement are demanding that American Negroes form themselves into power blocs, following the tradition of the Irish (who were originally subject to prejudice because of religion), the Italians, and the Poles. Both positions ignore the crucial difference between a minority thought of in terms of physique and one whose members can individually disappear into the general population as soon as they lose their distinguishing speech and other ethnic patterns of behavior. They also fail to consider the difference between coming from a civilization older than the civilization of the Western world and being the descendants of those who, at the time of contact, represented less complex cultures which were technologically overwhelmed. The Chinese, Japanese, and Jews were sustained by a sense of cultural superiority and difference, a high degree of endogamy, and the preservation of differences in behavior which served as breeding barriers and kept those who wished to act as members of minority groups together as groups. Even the American Indians after four centuries of contact can relate back to the locale of their historical past and preserve a certain degree of ethnic identity that is denied to those Americans who are the descendants of voluntary or involuntary immigrants.

The Negro American has no more cultural past than does the average white American whose ancestors have been in this country for eight or ten generations. He knows that some of his ancestors came from somewhere in Africa, as white Americans know or believe that all of their ancestors came from somewhere in Europe. But the majority of white Americans, with predominantly European ancestry, and the majority of Negro Americans, with European and some actual or imputed African ancestry, can actually draw only on American culture. The fact that European immigrants continued to come long after the slave trade ended obscures this fact somewhat, but in contrast to those groups who have preserved a connection between biological descent, country of origin, and ethnic identity, white and Negro Americans stand together, without the possibility of any legitimate pride except that which springs from their own achievements here. Invoking the history of Central African kingdoms to provide points of racial pride is as ridiculous as endowing the descendants of eastern or western Europeans with the achievements of Mediterranean history.

Yet as Americans, Negroes in the United States have the precedent of groups who organized along ethnic lines and achieved political power, freedom from discrimination, and a place in the sun. Too much emphasis on the spurious nature of racial classification by antisegregationists could backfire into emasculating the very necessary attempts to build up political responsibility, internal cohesion, and activism in Negro groups. Too much emphasis on race in political terms might lead to the complementary ridiculousness of the *Daily News* editorial (3) which accused Adam Clayton Powell of not really being a Negro but merely passing as one since, although he was reared as a Negro, he actually had three white grandparents.

So in giving careful biological definitions of strain, race and species, of Mendelian populations and breeding isolates, the responsible biologist must also be prepared to deal with contemporary social realities in the light of the kind of past social realities which Dr. Marshall so vividly outlined. If we are to keep a lively relationship between science and the promotion of human welfare, we need to cultivate an interchange between those working on the newest and most exciting problems of human biology, such as those outlined in Professor Baker's description of the International Biological Program, and those who are seeking by new methods of environmental change to alter relationships between human groups that have been fallaciously based on imputed biological differences.

As in all other endeavors based on scientific research, it is as important to state what we don't know as it is to clarify and expound what is currently believed to have been established. This was done during the question period at the end of Session II of the symposium. The question was asked: Why is a population with A, B, and O blood types better off than one with only A and O types? Neither Dr. Glass nor Dr. Mayr was able to give a definite answer to the question, and the suggestions each made of the possible answers were quite different.

Dr. Dobzhansky closed the question period by answering the question: "Should the scientist withhold information as well as opinion if these may have bad social implications?"

> I believe that information should not be withheld, but that does not absolve a scientist of responsibility for what misuses this information is subjected to. In other words, if I publish certain information, and I see that others are making out of this information what I regard as unjustified use, I would consider it my obligation to say that that particular use, I regard as misuse. I would say that it is not justified to say, "I am a scientist; I have produced information, and I am no longer interested in what happens after that." That sort of absolute impartiality I believe amounts to absolute irresponsibility, and in our world a scientist has no right to be irresponsible.

> I might add that to forbear bringing our scientific tools to focus on any aspect of this problem—scientifically, not pseudoscientifically— means to deny life to the relationship between science and the wellbeing of mankind. I agree with Professor Fried that sometimes the wellbeing of mankind has been used to cover the very worst purposes, but possibly we have to tolerate the expression of humanitarian intentions as an argument in favor of procedures that we decry in order to be sure that humanitarianism will in fact be allowed to develop in the world.

One of the questioners contributed a comment of an Englishman of letters: "Where it is a duty to worship the sun, it is fairly certain to be a crime to study the laws of heat." But the enemy's lip service to science and to humanitarianism makes it possible to encounter him on those grounds, if scientists and humanitarians are alert, and to counter his procedures by promoting a greater understanding of science.

Meanwhile, the price in human suffering, loss of human potential, and ethical damage that this country is paying because of such concepts as "average biological differences" applied to parts of our highly mixed and diversified populations is incalculable. A fuller understanding of the significance of the history of our unique species, our vicissitudes in time and place, and our inherent potentialities is an essential underpinning for dealing responsibly with our relationships one with another.

REFERENCES

1. Melville J. Herskovits, *The American Negro: A Study in Racial Crossing* (New York, Alfred A. Knopf, 1928).
2. W. Lloyd Warner, Buford H. Junker, Walter A. Adams, *Color and Human Nature: Negro Personality Development in a Northern City* (Washington, American Council on Education, 1941).
3. Editorial, New York *Daily News*, April 26, 1967.